Agile Data Science

Russell Jurney

Beijing · Cambridge · Farnham · Köln · Sebastopol · Tokyo

Agile Data Science

by Russell Jurney

Copyright © 2014 Data Syndrome LLC. All rights reserved.

Printed in the United States of America.

Published by O'Reilly Media, Inc., 1005 Gravenstein Highway North, Sebastopol, CA 95472.

O'Reilly books may be purchased for educational, business, or sales promotional use. Online editions are also available for most titles (*http://my.safaribooksonline.com*). For more information, contact our corporate/institutional sales department: 800-998-9938 or *corporate@oreilly.com*.

Editors: Mike Loukides and Mary Treseler	**Cover Designer:** Karen Montgomery
Production Editor: Nicole Shelby	**Interior Designer:** David Futato
Copyeditor: Rachel Monaghan	**Illustrator:** Kara Ebrahim
Proofreader: Linley Dolby	

October 2013:   First Edition

Revision History for the First Edition:

2013-10-11:   First release

See *http://oreilly.com/catalog/errata.csp?isbn=9781449326265* for release details.

ISBN: 978-1-449-32626-5

[LSI]

Table of Contents

Preface

I wrote this book to get over a failed project and to ensure that others do not repeat my mistakes. In this book, I draw from and reflect upon my experience building analytics applications at two Hadoop shops.

Agile Data Science has three goals: to provide a how-to guide for building analytics applications with big data using Hadoop; to help teams collaborate on big data projects in an agile manner; and to give structure to the practice of applying Agile Big Data analytics in a way that advances the field.

Who This Book Is For

Agile Data Science is a course to help big data beginners and budding data scientists to become productive members of data science and analytics teams. It aims to help engineers, analysts, and data scientists work with big data in an agile way using Hadoop. It introduces an agile methodology well suited for big data.

This book is targeted at programmers with some exposure to developing software and working with data. Designers and product managers might particularly enjoy Chapters 1, 2, and 5, which would serve as an introduction to the agile process without an excessive focus on running code.

Agile Data Science assumes you are working in a *nix environment. Examples for Windows users aren't available, but are possible via Cygwin. A user-contributed Linux Vagrant image with all the prerequisites installed is available here (*https://github.com/charlesflynn/agiledata*). You can quickly boot a Linux machine in VirtualBox using this tool.

How This Book Is Organized

This book is organized into two sections. Part I introduces the data- and toolset we will use in the tutorials in Part II. Part I is intentionally brief, taking only enough time to introduce the tools. We go more in-depth into their use in Part II, so don't worry if you're a little overwhelmed in Part I. The chapters that compose Part I are as follows:

Chapter 1, Theory
> Introduces the Agile Big Data methodology.

Chapter 2, Data
> Describes the dataset used in this book, and the mechanics of a simple prediction.

Chapter 3, Agile Tools
> Introduces our toolset, and helps you get it up and running on your own machine.

Chapter 4, To the Cloud!
> Walks you through scaling the tools in Chapter 3 to petabyte scale using the cloud.

Part II is a tutorial in which we build an analytics application using Agile Big Data. It is a notebook-style guide to building an analytics application. We climb the data-value pyramid one level at a time, applying agile principles as we go. I'll demonstrate a way of building value step by step in small, agile iterations. Part II comprises the following chapters:

Chapter 5, Collecting and Displaying Records
> Helps you download your inbox and then connect or "plumb" emails through to a web application.

Chapter 6, Visualizing Data with Charts
> Steps you through how to navigate your data by preparing simple charts in a web application.

Chapter 7, Exploring Data with Reports
> Teaches you how to extract entities from your data and link between them to create interactive reports.

Chapter 8, Making Predictions
> Helps you use what you've done so far to infer the response rate to emails.

Chapter 9, Driving Actions
> Explains how to extend your predictions into a real-time ensemble classifier to help make emails that will be replied to.

Conventions Used in This Book

The following typographical conventions are used in this book:

Italic
> Indicates new terms, URLs, email addresses, filenames, and file extensions.

`Constant width`

Used for program listings, as well as within paragraphs to refer to program elements such as variable or function names, databases, data types, environment variables, statements, and keywords.

`Constant width bold`

Shows commands or other text that should be typed literally by the user.

`Constant width italic`

Shows text that should be replaced with user-supplied values or by values determined by context.

 This icon signifies a tip, suggestion, or general note.

 This icon indicates a warning or caution.

Using Code Examples

Supplemental material (code examples, exercises, etc.) is available for download at *https://github.com/rjurney/Agile_Data_Code*.

This book is here to help you get your job done. In general, if example code is offered with this book, you may use it in your programs and documentation. You do not need to contact us for permission unless you're reproducing a significant portion of the code. For example, writing a program that uses several chunks of code from this book does not require permission. Selling or distributing a CD-ROM of examples from O'Reilly books does require permission. Answering a question by citing this book and quoting example code does not require permission. Incorporating a significant amount of example code from this book into your product's documentation does require permission.

We appreciate, but do not require, attribution. An attribution usually includes the title, author, publisher, and ISBN. For example: "*Agile Data Science* by Russell Jurney (O'Reilly). Copyright 2014 Data Syndrome LLC, 978-1-449-32626-5."

If you feel your use of code examples falls outside fair use or the permission given above, feel free to contact us at *permissions@oreilly.com*.

Safari® Books Online

 Safari Books Online (*www.safaribooksonline.com*) is an on-demand digital library that delivers expert content in both book and video form from the world's leading authors in technology and business.

Technology professionals, software developers, web designers, and business and creative professionals use Safari Books Online as their primary resource for research, problem solving, learning, and certification training.

Safari Books Online offers a range of product mixes and pricing programs for organizations, government agencies, and individuals. Subscribers have access to thousands of books, training videos, and prepublication manuscripts in one fully searchable database from publishers like O'Reilly Media, Prentice Hall Professional, Addison-Wesley Professional, Microsoft Press, Sams, Que, Peachpit Press, Focal Press, Cisco Press, John Wiley & Sons, Syngress, Morgan Kaufmann, IBM Redbooks, Packt, Adobe Press, FT Press, Apress, Manning, New Riders, McGraw-Hill, Jones & Bartlett, Course Technology, and dozens more. For more information about Safari Books Online, please visit us online.

How to Contact Us

Please address comments and questions concerning this book to the publisher:

O'Reilly Media, Inc.
1005 Gravenstein Highway North
Sebastopol, CA 95472
800-998-9938 (in the United States or Canada)
707-829-0515 (international or local)
707-829-0104 (fax)

We have a web page for this book, where we list errata, examples, and any additional information. You can access this page at *http://oreil.ly/agile-data-science*.

To comment or ask technical questions about this book, send email to *bookquestions@oreilly.com*.

For more information about our books, courses, conferences, and news, see our website at *http://www.oreilly.com*.

Find us on Facebook: *http://facebook.com/oreilly*

Follow us on Twitter: *http://twitter.com/oreillymedia*

Watch us on YouTube: *http://www.youtube.com/oreillymedia*

Setup

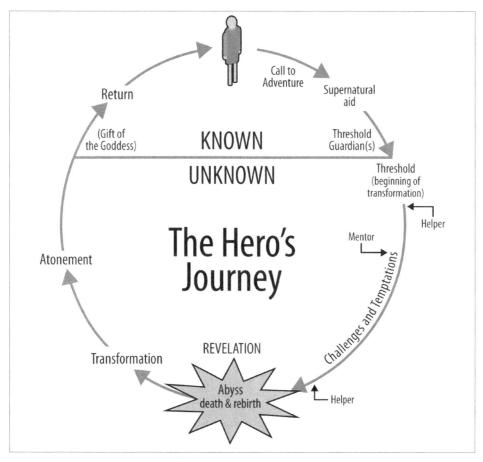

Figure I.1. The Hero's Journey, from Wikipedia

## CHAPTER 1

Theory

We are uncovering better ways of developing software by doing it and helping others do it. Through this work we have come to value:

Individuals and interactions over processes and tools
Working software over comprehensive documentation
Customer collaboration over contract negotiation
Responding to change over following a plan

That is, while there is value in the items on the right, we value the items on the left more.

—The Agile Manifesto

Agile Big Data

Agile Big Data is a development methodology that copes with the unpredictable realities of creating analytics applications from data at scale. It is a guide for operating the Hadoop data refinery to harness the power of big data.

Warehouse-scale computing has given us enormous storage and compute resources to solve new kinds of problems involving storing and processing unprecedented amounts of data. There is great interest in bringing new tools to bear on formerly intractable problems, to derive entirely new products from raw data, to refine raw data into profitable insight, and to productize and productionize insight in new kinds of analytics applications. These tools are processor cores and disk spindles, paired with visualization, statistics, and machine learning. This is *data science*.

At the same time, during the last 20 years, the World Wide Web has emerged as the dominant medium for information exchange. During this time, software engineering has been transformed by the "agile" revolution in how applications are conceived, built, and maintained. These new processes bring in more projects and products on time and under budget, and enable small teams or single actors to develop entire applications spanning broad domains. This is *agile software development*.

But there's a problem. Working with real data in the wild, doing data science, and performing serious research takes time—longer than an agile cycle (on the order of months). It takes more time than is available in many organizations for a project sprint, meaning today's applied researcher is more than pressed for time. Data science is stuck on the old-school software schedule known as the *waterfall method*.

Our problem and our opportunity come at the intersection of these two trends: how can we incorporate data science, which is applied research and requires exhaustive effort on an unpredictable timeline, into the agile application? How can analytics applications do better than the waterfall method that we've long left behind? How can we craft applications for unknown, evolving data models?

This book attempts to synthesize two fields, agile development and big data science, to meld research and engineering into a productive relationship. To achieve this, it presents a lightweight toolset that can cope with the uncertain, shifting sea of raw data. The book goes on to show you how to iteratively build value using this stack, to get back to agility and mine data to turn it to dollars.

Agile Big Data aims to put you back in the driver's seat, ensuring that your applied research produces useful products that meet the needs of real users.

Big Words Defined

Scalability, *NoSQL*, *cloud computing*, *big data*—these are all controversial terms. Here, they are defined as they pertain to Agile Big Data:

Scalability

> This is the simplicity with which you can grow or shrink some operation in response to demand. In Agile Big Data, it means software tools and techniques that grow sublinearly in terms of cost and complexity as load and complexity in an application grow linearly. We use the same tools for data, large and small, and we embrace a methodology that lets us build once, rather than re-engineer continuously.

NoSQL

> Short for "Not only SQL," this means escaping the bounds imposed by storing structured data in monolithic relational databases. It means going beyond tools that were optimized for Online Transaction Processing (OLTP) and extended to Online Analytic Processing (OLAP) to use a broader set of tools that are better suited to viewing data in terms of analytic structures and algorithms. It means escaping the bounds of a single machine with expensive storage and starting out with concurrent systems that will grow linearly as users and load increase. It means not hitting a wall as soon as our database gets bogged down, and then struggling to tune, shard, and mitigate problems continuously.

The NoSQL tools we'll be using are *Hadoop,* a highly parallel batch-processing system, and *MongoDB,* a distributed document store.

Cloud computing

Computing on the cloud means employing infrastructure as a service from providers like Amazon Web Services to compose applications at the level of data center as computer. As application developers, we use cloud computing to avoid getting bogged down in the details of infrastructure while building applications that scale.

Big data

There is a market around the belief that enormous value will be extracted from the ever-increasing pile of transaction logs being aggregated by the mission-critical systems of today and tomorrow; that's Big Data. Big Data systems use local storage, commodity server hardware, and free and open source software to cheaply process data at a scale where it becomes feasible to work with atomic records that are voluminously logged and processed.

 Eric Tschetter, cofounder and lead architect at Metamarkets, says this about NoSQL in practice:

> "I define NoSQL as the movement towards use-case specialized storage and query layer combinations. The RDBMS is a highly generic weapon that can be utilized to solve any data storage and query need up to a certain amount of load. I see NoSQL as a move toward other types of storage architectures that are optimized for a specific use-case and can offer benefits in areas like operational complexity by making assumptions about said use cases."

Agile Big Data Teams

Products are built by teams of people, and agile methods focus on people over process, so Agile Big Data starts with a team.

Data science is a broad discipline, spanning analysis, design, development, business, and research. The roles of Agile Big Data team members, defined in a spectrum from customer to operations, look something like Figure 1-1:

Customer	Business Development	Marketer	Product Manager	Experience Designer	Interaction Designer	Web Developer	Engineer	Data Scientist	Researcher	Platform Engineer	DevOps Engineer

Figure 1-1. The roles in an Agile Big Data team

These roles can be defined as:

- **Customers** use your product, click your buttons and links, or ignore you completely. Your job is to create value for them repeatedly. Their interest determines the success of your product.

- **Business development** signs early customers, either firsthand or through the creation of landing pages and promotion. Delivers traction from product in market.

- **Marketers** talk to customers to determine which markets to pursue. They determine the starting perspective from which an Agile Big Data product begins.

- **Product managers** take in the perspectives of each role, synthesizing them to build consensus about the vision and direction of the product.

- **Userexperience designers** are responsible for fitting the design around the data to match the perspective of the customer. This role is critical, as the output of statistical models can be difficult to interpret by "normal" users who have no concept of the semantics of the model's output (i.e., how can something be 75% true?).

- **Interaction designers** design interactions around data models so users find their value.

- **Web developers** create the web applications that deliver data to a web browser.

- **Engineers** build the systems that deliver data to applications.

- **Data scientists** explore and transform data in novel ways to create and publish new features and combine data from diverse sources to create new value. Data scientists make visualizations with researchers, engineers, web developers, and designers to expose raw, intermediate, and refined data early and often.

- **Applied researchers** solve the heavy problems that data scientists uncover and that stand in the way of delivering value. These problems take intense focus and time and require novel methods from statistics and machine learning.

- **Platform engineers** solve problems in the distributed infrastructure that enable Agile Big Data at scale to proceed without undue pain. Platform engineers handle work tickets for immediate blocking bugs and implement long-term plans and projects to maintain and improve usability for researchers, data scientists, and engineers.

- **Operations/DevOps professionals** ensure smooth setup and operation of production data infrastructure. They automate deployment and take pages when things go wrong.

Recognizing the Opportunity and Problem

The broad skillset needed to build data products presents both an opportunity and a problem. If these skills can be brought to bear by experts in each role working as a team on a rich dataset, problems can be decomposed into parts and directly attacked. Data science is then an efficient assembly line, as illustrated in Figure 1-2.

However, as team size increases to satisfy the need for expertise in these diverse areas, communication overhead quickly dominates. A researcher who is eight persons away from customers is unlikely to solve relevant problems and more likely to solve arcane problems. Likewise, team meetings of a dozen individuals are unlikely to be productive. We might split this team into multiple departments and establish contracts of delivery between them, but then we lose both agility and cohesion. Waiting on the output of research, we invent specifications and soon we find ourselves back in the waterfall method.

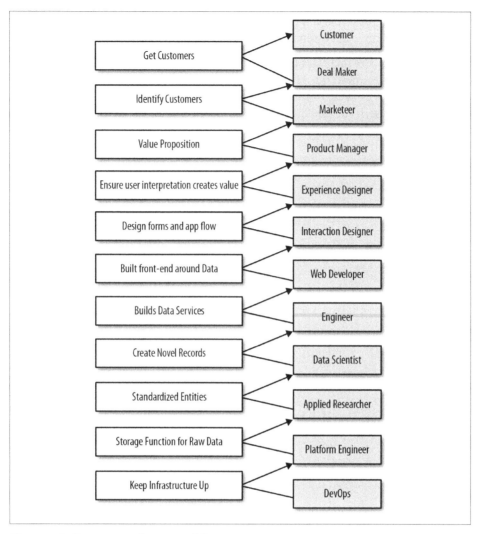

Figure 1-2. Expert contributor workflow

And yet we know that agility and a cohesive vision and consensus about a product are essential to our success in building products. The worst product problem is one team working on more than one vision. How are we to reconcile the increased span of expertise and the disjoint timelines of applied research, data science, software development, and design?

Adapting to Change

To remain agile, we must embrace and adapt to these new conditions. We must adopt changes in line with lean methodologies to stay productive.

Several changes in particular make a return to agility possible:

- Choosing generalists over specialists
- Preferring small teams over large teams
- Using high-level tools and platforms: cloud computing, distributed systems, and platforms as a service (PaaS)
- Continuous and iterative sharing of intermediate work, even when that work may be incomplete

In Agile Big Data, a small team of generalists uses scalable, high-level tools and cloud computing to iteratively refine data into increasingly higher states of value. We embrace a software stack leveraging cloud computing, distributed systems, and platforms as a service. Then we use this stack to iteratively publish the intermediate results of even our most in-depth research to snowball value from simple records to predictions and actions that create value and let us capture some of it to turn data into dollars. Let's examine each item in detail.

Harnessing the power of generalists

In Agile Big Data we value generalists over specialists, as shown in Figure 1-3.

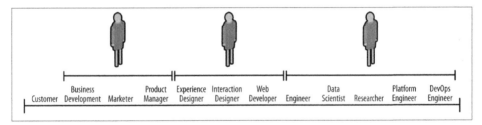

Figure 1-3. Broad roles in an Agile Big Data team

In other words, we measure the breadth of teammates' skills as much as the depth of their knowledge and their talent in any one area. Examples of good Agile Big Data team members include:

- Designers who deliver working CSS
- Web developers who build entire applications and understand user interface and experience
- Data scientists capable of both research and building web services and applications
- Researchers who check in working source code, explain results, and share intermediate data
- Product managers able to understand the nuances in all areas

Design in particular is a critical role on the Agile Big Data team. Design does not end with appearance or experience. Design encompasses all aspects of the product, from architecture, distribution, and user experience to work environment.

 In the documentary *The Lost Interview*, Steve Jobs said this about design: "Designing a product is keeping five thousand things in your brain and fitting them all together in new and different ways to get what you want. And every day you discover something new that is a new problem or a new opportunity to fit these things together a little differently. And it's that process that is the magic."

Leveraging agile platforms

In Agile Big Data, we use the easiest-to-use, most approachable distributed systems, along with cloud computing and platforms as a service, to minimize infrastructure costs and maximize productivity. The simplicity of our stack helps enable a return to agility. We'll use this stack to compose scalable systems in as few steps as possible. This lets us move fast and consume all available data without running into scalability problems that cause us to discard data or remake our application in flight. That is to say, *we only build it once*.

Sharing intermediate results

Finally, to address the very real differences in timelines between researchers and data scientists and the rest of the team, we adopt a sort of *data collage* as our mechanism of mending these disjointed scales. In other words, we piece our app together from the abundance of views, visualizations, and properties that form the "menu" for our application.

Researchers and data scientists, who work on longer timelines than agile sprints typically allow, generate data daily—albeit not in a "publishable" state. In Agile Big Data, there is no unpublishable state. The rest of the team must see weekly, if not daily (or more often), updates in the state of the data. This kind of engagement with researchers is essential to unifying the team and enabling product management.

That means publishing intermediate results—incomplete data, the scraps of analysis. These "clues" keep the team united, and as these results become interactive, everyone becomes informed as to the true nature of the data, the progress of the research, and how to combine clues into features of value. Development and design must proceed from this shared reality. The audience for these continuous releases can start small and grow as they become presentable (as shown in Figure 1-4), but customers must be included quickly.

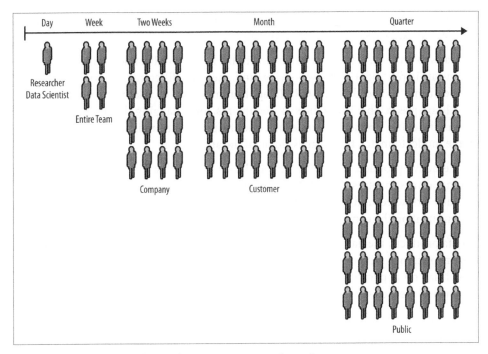

Figure 1-4. Growing audience from conception to launch

Agile Big Data Process

The Agile Big Data process embraces the iterative nature of data science and the efficiency our tools enable to build and extract increasing levels of structure and value from our data.

Given the spectrum of skills within a data product team, the possibilities are endless. With the team spanning so many disciplines, building web products is inherently collaborative. To collaborate, teams need direction: every team member passionately and stubbornly pursuing a common goal. To get that direction, you require consensus.

Building and maintaining consensus while collaborating is the hardest part of building software. The principal risk in software product teams is building to different blueprints. Clashing visions result in incohesive holes that sink products.

Applications are sometimes *mocked* before they are built: product managers conduct market research, while designers iterate mocks with feedback from prospective users. These mocks serve as a common blueprint for the team.

Real-world requirements shift as we learn from our users and conditions change, even when the data is static. So our blueprints must change with time. Agile methods were created to facilitate implementation of evolving requirements, and to replace mockups with real working systems as soon as possible.

Typical web products—those driven by forms backed by predictable, constrained transaction data in relational databases—have fundamentally different properties than products featuring mined data. In CRUD applications, data is relatively consistent. The models are predictable SQL tables or documents, and changing them is a product decision. The data's "opinion" is irrelevant, and the product team is free to impose its will on the model to match the business logic of the application.

In interactive products driven by mined data, none of that holds. Real data is dirty. Mining always involves dirt. If the data isn't dirty, it wouldn't be data mining. Even carefully extracted and refined mined information can be fuzzy and unpredictable. Presenting it on the consumer Internet requires long labor and great care.

In data products, the data is ruthlessly opinionated. Whatever we wish the data to say, it is unconcerned with our own opinions. It says what it says. This means the waterfall model has no application. It also means that mocks are an insufficient blueprint to establish consensus in software teams.

Mocks of data products are a specification of the application without its essential character, the true value of the information being presented. Mocks as blueprints make assumptions about complex data models they have no reasonable basis for. When specifying lists of recommendations, mocks often mislead. When mocks specify full-blown interactions, they do more than that: they suppress reality and promote assumption. And yet we know that good design and user experience are about minimizing assumption. What are we to do?

The goal of agile product development is to identify the essential character of an application and to build that up first before adding features. This imparts agility to the project, making it more likely to satisfy its real, essential requirements as they evolve. In data products, that essential character will surprise you. If it doesn't, you are either doing it wrong, or your data isn't very interesting. Information has context, and when that context is interactive, insight is not predictable.

Code Review and Pair Programming

To avoid systemic errors, data scientists share their code with the rest of the team on a regular basis, so code review is important. It is easy to fix errors in parsing that hide systemic errors in algorithms. *Pair programming*, where pairs of data hackers go over code line by line, checking its output and explaining the semantics, can help detect these errors.

Agile Environments: Engineering Productivity

Rows of cubicles like cells of a hive. Overbooked
conference rooms camped and decamped.
Microsoft Outlook a modern punchcard.
Monolithic insanity. A sea of cubes.

Deadlines interrupted by oscillating cacophonies
of rumors shouted, spread like waves
uninterrupted by naked desks. Headphone
budgets. Not working, close together. Decibel
induced telecommuting. The open plan.

Competing monstrosities seeking productivity but
not finding it.

—Poem by author

Generalists require more uninterrupted concentration and quiet than do specialists. That is because the context of their work is broader, and therefore their immersion is deeper. Their environment must suit this need.

Invest in two to three times the space of a typical cube farm, or you are wasting your people. In this setup, some people don't need desks, which drives costs down.

We can do better. We should do better. It costs more, but it is inexpensive.

In Agile Big Data, we recognize team members as creative workers, not office workers. We therefore structure our environment more like a studio than an office. At the same time, we recognize that employing advanced mathematics on data to build products requires quiet contemplation and intense focus. So we incorporate elements of the library as well.

> Many enterprises limit their productivity enhancement of employees to the acquisition of skills. However, about 86% of productivity problems reside in the work environment of organizations. The work environment has effect on the performance of employees. The type of work environment in which employees operate determines the way in which such enterprises prosper.
>
> —Akinyele Samuel Taiwo

> It is much higher cost to employ people than it is to maintain and operate a building, hence spending money on improving the work environment is the most cost effective way of improving productivity because of small percentage increase in productivity of 0.1% to 2% can have dramatic effects on the profitability of the company.
>
> —Derek Clements-Croome and Li Baizhan

Creative workers need three kinds of spaces to collaborate and build together. From open to closed, they are: collaboration space, personal space, and private space.

Collaboration Space

Collaboration space is where ideas are hatched. Situated along main thoroughfares and between departments, collaborative spaces are bright, open, comfortable, and inviting. They have no walls. They are flexible and reconfigurable. They are ever-changing, always being rearranged, and full of bean bags, pillows, and comfortable chairs. Collaboration space is where you feel the energy of your company: laughter, big conversations, excited voices talking over one another. Invest in and showcase these areas. Real, not plastic, plants keep sound from carrying—and they make air!

Private Space

Private space is where deadlines get met. Enclosed and soundproof, private spaces are libraries. There is no talking. Private space minimizes distractions: think dim light and white noise. There are bean bags, couches, and chairs, but ergonomics demand proper workstations too. These spaces might include separate sit/stand desks with docking stations behind (bead) curtains with 30-inch customized LCDs.

Personal Space

Personal space is where people call home. In between collaboration and private space in its degree of openness, personal space should be personalized by each individual to suit his or her needs (e.g., shared office or open desks, half or whole cube). Personal space should come with a menu and a budget. Themes and plant life should be encouraged. This is where some people will spend most of their time. On the other hand, given adequate collaborative and private space, a notebook, and a mobile device, some people don't need personal space at all.

Above all, the goal of the agile environment is to create immersion in data through the physical environment: printouts, posters, books, whiteboard, and more, as shown in Figure 1-5.

Figure 1-5. Data immersion through collage

Realizing Ideas with Large-Format Printing

Easy access to large-format printing is a requirement for the agile environment. Visualization in material form encourages sharing, collage, expressiveness, and creativity.

The HP DesignJet 111 is a 24-inch-wide large format printer that costs less than $1,000. Continuous ink delivery systems are available for less than $100 that bring the operational cost of large-format printing—for instance, 24 × 36 inch posters—to less than one dollar per poster.

At this price point, there is no excuse not to give a data team easy access to several large-format printers for both plain-paper proofs and glossy prints. It is very easy to get people excited about data across departments when they can see concrete proof of the progress of the data science team.

## CHAPTER 2

Data

This chapter introduces the dataset we will work on in the rest of the book: your own email inbox. It will also cover the kinds of tools we'll be using, and our reasoning for doing so. Finally, it will outline multiple perspectives we'll use in analyzing data for you to think about moving forward.

The book starts with data because in Agile Big Data, our process starts with the data.

 If you do not have a Gmail account, you will need to create one (at *http://mail.google.com*) and populate it with some email messages in order to complete the exercises in this chapter.

Email

Email is a fundamental part of the Internet. More than that, it is foundational, forming the basis for authentication for the Web and social networks. In addition to being abundant and well understood, email is complex, is rich in signal, and yields interesting information when mined.

We will be using your own email inbox as the dataset for the application we'll develop in order to make the examples relevant. By downloading your Gmail inbox and then using it in the examples, we will immediately face a "big" or actually, a "medium" data problem—processing the data on your local machine is just barely feasible. Working with data too large to fit in RAM this way requires that we use scalable tools, which is helpful as a learning device. By using your own email inbox, we'll enable insights into your own little world, helping you see which techniques are effective! This is cultivating *data intuition*, a major theme in Agile Big Data.

In this book, we use the same tools that you would use at petabyte scale, but in local mode on your own machine. This is more than an efficient way to process data; our choice of tools ensures that we only have to build it once, and it will scale up. This imparts simplicity on everything that we do and enables agility.

Working with Raw Data

Raw Email

Email's format is rigorously defined in IETF RFC-5322 (Request For Comments by the Internet Engineering Taskforce). To view a raw email in Gmail, select a message and then select the "show original" option in the top-right drop-down menu (Figure 2-1).

Figure 2-1. Gmail "show original" option

A raw email looks like this:

```
From: Russell Jurney <russell.jurney@gmail.com>
Mime-Version: 1.0 (1.0)
Date: Mon, 28 Nov 2011 14:57:38 -0800
Delivered-To: russell.jurney@gmail.com
Message-ID: <4484555894252760987@unknownmsgid>
Subject: Re: Lawn
To: William Jurney <******@hotmail.com>
Content-Type: text/plain; charset=ISO-8859-1

Dad, get a sack of Rye grass seed and plant it over there now.  It
will build up a nice turf over the winter, then die off when it warms
up.  Making for good topsoil you can plant regular grass in.

Will keep the weeds from taking over.

Russell Jurney datasyndrome.com
```

This is called *semistructured data.*

Structured Versus Semistructured Data

Wikipedia defines semistructured data as:

A form of structured data that does not conform with the formal structure of tables and data models associated with relational databases but nonetheless contains tags or other markers to separate semantic elements and enforce hierarchies of records and fields within the data.

This is in contrast to relational, structured data, which breaks data up into rigorously defined schemas before analytics begin for more efficient querying therafter. A structured view of email is demonstrated in the Berkeley Enron dataset by Andrew Fiore and Jeff Heer, shown in Figure 2-2.

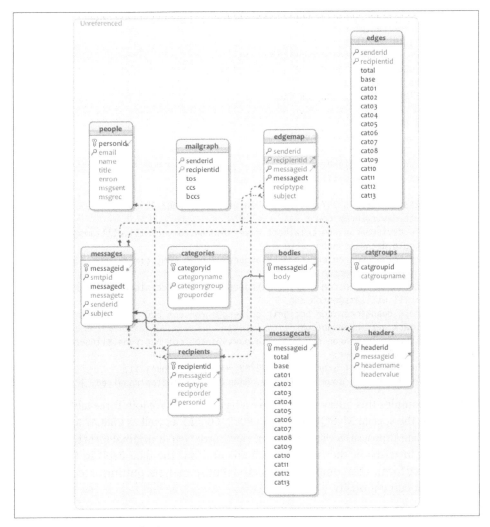

Figure 2-2. Enron email schema

SQL

To query a relational, structured schema, we typically use declarative programming languages like SQL. In SQL, we specify what we want, rather than what to do. This is different than declarative programming. In SQL, we specify the desired output rather than a set of operations on our data. A SQL query against the Enron relational email dataset to retrieve a single email in its entirety looks like this:

```
select m.smtpid as id,
    m.messagedt as date,
    s.email as sender,
    (select GROUP_CONCAT(CONCAT(r.reciptype, ':', p.email) SEPARATOR ' ')
        from recipients r
        join people p
            on r.personid=p.personid
        where r.messageid = 511) as to_cc_bcc,
    m.subject as subject,
    SUBSTR(b.body, 1, 200) as body
    from messages m
    join people s
        on m.senderid=s.personid
    join bodies b
        on m.messageid=b.messageid
    where m.messageid=511;
```

```
| <25772535.1075839951307.JavaMail.evans@thyme> | 2002-02-02 12:56:33
    | pete.davis@enron.com |
  to:pete.davis@enron.com cc:albert.meyers@enron.com cc:bill.williams@enron.com
    cc:craig.dean@enron.com
  cc:geir.solberg@enron.com cc:john.anderson@enron.com cc:mark.guzman@enron.com
    cc:michael.mier@enron.com
  cc:pete.davis@enron.com cc:ryan.slinger@enron.com bcc:albert.meyers@enron.com
    bcc:bill.williams@enron.com
  bcc:craig.dean@enron.com bcc:geir.solberg@enron.com bcc:john.anderson@enron.com
    bcc:mark.guzman@enron.com
  bcc:michael.mier@enron.com bcc:pete.davis@enron.com bcc:ryan.slinger@enron.com
    | Schedule Crawler:
  HourAhead Failure | Start Date: 2/2/02; HourAhead hour: 11;
  HourAhead schedule download failed. Manual intervention required. |
```

Note how complex this query is to retrieve a basic record. We join three tables and use a subquery, the special MySQL function GROUP_CONCAT as well as CONCAT and SUBSTR. Relational data almost discourages us from viewing data in its original form by requiring us to think in terms of the relational schema and not the data itself in its original, denormalized form. This complexity affects our entire analysis, putting us in "SQL land" instead of document reality.

Also note that defining the preceding tables is complex in and of itself:

```
CREATE TABLE bodies (
  messageid int(10) unsigned NOT NULL default '0',
```

```sql
  body text,
  PRIMARY KEY  (messageid)
) TYPE=MyISAM;

CREATE TABLE categories (
  categoryid int(10) unsigned NOT NULL auto_increment,
  categoryname varchar(255) default NULL,
  categorygroup int(10) unsigned default NULL,
  grouporder int(10) unsigned default NULL,
  PRIMARY KEY  (categoryid),
  KEY categories_categorygroup (categorygroup)
) TYPE=MyISAM;

CREATE TABLE catgroups (
  catgroupid int(10) unsigned NOT NULL default '0',
  catgroupname varchar(255) default NULL,
  PRIMARY KEY  (catgroupid)
) TYPE=MyISAM;

CREATE TABLE edgemap (
  senderid int(10) unsigned default NULL,
  recipientid int(10) unsigned default NULL,
  messageid int(10) unsigned default NULL,
  messagedt timestamp(14) NOT NULL,
  reciptype enum('bcc','cc','to') default NULL,
  subject varchar(255) default NULL,
  KEY senderid (senderid,recipientid),
  KEY messageid (messageid),
  KEY messagedt (messagedt),
  KEY senderid_2 (senderid),
  KEY recipientid (recipientid)
) TYPE=MyISAM;

CREATE TABLE edges (
  senderid int(10) unsigned default NULL,
  recipientid int(10) unsigned default NULL,
  total int(10) unsigned NOT NULL default '0',
  base int(10) unsigned NOT NULL default '0',
  cat01 int(10) unsigned NOT NULL default '0',
  cat02 int(10) unsigned NOT NULL default '0',
  cat03 int(10) unsigned NOT NULL default '0',
  cat04 int(10) unsigned NOT NULL default '0',
  cat05 int(10) unsigned NOT NULL default '0',
  cat06 int(10) unsigned NOT NULL default '0',
  cat07 int(10) unsigned NOT NULL default '0',
  cat08 int(10) unsigned NOT NULL default '0',
  cat09 int(10) unsigned NOT NULL default '0',
  cat10 int(10) unsigned NOT NULL default '0',
  cat11 int(10) unsigned NOT NULL default '0',
  cat12 int(10) unsigned NOT NULL default '0',
  cat13 int(10) unsigned NOT NULL default '0',
  UNIQUE KEY senderid (senderid,recipientid)
```

```
) TYPE=MyISAM;

CREATE TABLE headers (
  headerid int(10) unsigned NOT NULL auto_increment,
  messageid int(10) unsigned default NULL,
  headername varchar(255) default NULL,
  headervalue text,
  PRIMARY KEY  (headerid),
  KEY headers_headername (headername),
  KEY headers_messageid (messageid)
) TYPE=MyISAM;

CREATE TABLE messages (
  messageid int(10) unsigned NOT NULL auto_increment,
  smtpid varchar(255) default NULL,
  messagedt timestamp(14) NOT NULL,
  messagetz varchar(20) default NULL,
  senderid int(10) unsigned default NULL,
  subject varchar(255) default NULL,
  PRIMARY KEY  (messageid),
  UNIQUE KEY smtpid (smtpid),
  KEY messages_senderid (senderid),
  KEY messages_subject (subject)
) TYPE=MyISAM;

CREATE TABLE people (
  personid int(10) unsigned NOT NULL auto_increment,
  email varchar(255) default NULL,
  name varchar(255) default NULL,
  title varchar(255) default NULL,
  enron tinyint(3) unsigned default NULL,
  msgsent int(10) unsigned default NULL,
  msgrec int(10) unsigned default NULL,
  PRIMARY KEY  (personid),
  UNIQUE KEY email (email)
) TYPE=MyISAM;
--
--

CREATE TABLE recipients (
  recipientid int(10) unsigned NOT NULL auto_increment,
  messageid int(10) unsigned default NULL,
  reciptype enum('bcc','cc','to') default NULL,
  reciporder int(10) unsigned default NULL,
  personid int(10) unsigned default NULL,
  PRIMARY KEY  (recipientid),
  KEY messageid (messageid)
) TYPE=MyISAM;
```

By contrast, in Agile Big Data we use dataflow languages to define the form of our data in code, and then we publish it directly to a document store without ever formally specifying a schema! This is optimized for our process: doing data science, where we're deriving new information from existing data. There is no benefit to externally specifying schemas in this context—it is pure overhead. After all, we don't know what we'll wind up with until it's ready! Data science will always surprise.

However, relational structure does have benefits. We can see what time users send emails very easily with a simple select/group by/order query:

```
select senderid as id,
    hour(messagedt) as sent_hour,
    count(*)
    from messages
    where senderid=511
    group by
        senderid,
        m_hour
    order by
        senderid,
        m_hour;
```

which results in this simple table:

```
+----------+--------+----------+
| senderid | m_hour | count(*) |
+----------+--------+----------+
|        1 |      0 |        4 |
|        1 |      1 |        3 |
|        1 |      3 |        2 |
|        1 |      5 |        1 |
|        1 |      8 |        3 |
|        1 |      9 |        1 |
|        1 |     10 |        5 |
|        1 |     11 |        2 |
|        1 |     12 |        2 |
|        1 |     14 |        1 |
|        1 |     15 |        5 |
|        1 |     16 |        4 |
|        1 |     17 |        1 |
|        1 |     19 |        1 |
|        1 |     20 |        1 |
|        1 |     21 |        1 |
|        1 |     22 |        1 |
|        1 |     23 |        1 |
+----------+--------+----------+
```

Relational databases split data up into tables according to its structure and precompute indexes for operating between these tables. Indexes enable these systems to be responsive on a single computer. Declarative programming is used to query this structure.

This kind of declarative programming is ideally suited to consuming and querying structured data in aggregate to produce simple charts and figures. When we know what we want, we can efficiently tell the SQL engine what that is, and it will compute the relations for us. We don't have to worry about the details of the query's execution.

NoSQL

In contrast to SQL, when building analytics applications we often don't know the query we want to run. Much experimentation and iteration is required to arrive at the solution to any given problem. Data is often unavailable in a relational format. Data in the wild is not normalized; it is fuzzy and dirty. Extracting structure is a lengthy process that we perform iteratively as we process data for different features.

For these reasons, in Agile Big Data we primarily employ imperative languages against distributed systems. Imperative languages like Pig Latin describe steps to manipulate data in pipelines. Rather than precompute indexes against structure we don't yet have, we use many processing cores in parallel to read individual records. Hadoop and work queues make this possible.

In addition to mapping well to technologies like Hadoop, which enables us to easily scale our processing, imperative languages put the focus of our tools where most of the work in building analytics applications is: in one or two hard-won, key steps where we do clever things that deliver most of the value of our application.

Compared to writing SQL queries, arriving at these clever operations is a lengthy and often exhaustive process, as we employ techniques from statistics, machine learning, and social network analysis. Thus, imperative programming fits the task.

To summarize, when schemas are rigorous, and SQL is our lone tool, our perspective comes to be dominated by tools optimized for consumption, rather than mining data. Rigorously defined schemas get in the way. Our ability to connect intuitively with the data is inhibited. Working with semistructured data, on the other hand, enables us to focus on the data directly, manipulating it iteratively to extract value and to transform it to a product form. In Agile Big Data, we embrace NoSQL for what it enables us to do.

Serialization

Although we can work with semistructured data as pure text, it is still helpful to impose some kind of structure to the raw records using a schema. Serialization systems give us this functionality. Available serialization systems include the following:

> Thrift: *http://thrift.apache.org/*
> Protobuf: *http://code.google.com/p/protobuf/*
> Avro: *http://avro.apache.org/*

Although it is the least mature of these options, we'll choose Avro. Avro allows complex data structures, it includes a schema with each file, and it has support in Apache Pig. Installing Avro is easy, and it requires no external service to run.

We'll define a single, simple Avro schema for an email document as defined in RFC-5322. It is well and good to define a schema up front, but in practice, much processing will be required to extract all the entities in that schema. So our initial schema might look very simple, like this:

```
{
    "type":"record",
    "name":"RawEmail",
    "fields":
    [
        {
            "name":"thread_id",
            "type":["string", "null"],
            "doc":""
        },
        {
            "name":"raw_email",
            "type": ["string", "null"]
        }
    ]
}
```

We might extract only a `thread_id` as a unique identifier, and then store the entire raw email string in a field on its own. If a unique identifier is not easy to extract from raw records, we can generate a UUID (universally unique identifier) and add it as a field.

Our job as we process data, then, is to add fields to our schema as we extract them, all the while retaining the raw data in its own field if we can. We can always go back to the mother source.

Extracting and Exposing Features in Evolving Schemas

As Pete Warden notes in his talk "Embracing the Chaos of Data", (*http://bit.ly/171ulz7*) most freely available data is crude and unstructured. It is the availability of huge volumes of such ugly data, and not carefully cleaned and normalized tables, that makes it "big data." Therein lies the opportunity in mining crude data into refined information, and using that information to drive new kinds of actions.

Extracted features from unstructured data get cleaned only in the harsh light of day, as users consume them and complain; if you can't ship your features as you extract them, you're in a state of free fall. The hardest part of building data products is pegging entity and feature extraction to products smaller than your ultimate vision. This is why schemas must start as blobs of unstructured text and evolve into structured data only as features are extracted.

Features must be exposed in some product form as they are created, or they will never achieve a product-ready state. Derived data that lives in the basement of your product is unlikely to shape up. It is better to create entity pages to bring entities up to a "consumer-grade" form, to incrementally improve these entities, and to progressively combine them than to try to expose myriad derived data in a grand vision from the get-go.

While mining data into well-structured information, using that information to expose new facts and make predictions that enable actions offers enormous potential for value creation. Data is brutal and unforgiving, and failing to mind its true nature will dash the dreams of the most ambitious product manager.

As we'll see throughout the book, schemas evolve and improve, and so do features that expose them. When they evolve concurrently, we are truly agile.

Data Pipelines

We'll be working with semistructured data in data pipelines to extract and display its different features. The advantage of working with data in this way is that we don't invest time in extracting structure unless it is of interest and use to us. Thus, in the principles of KISS (Keep It Simple, Stupid!) and YAGNI (You Ain't Gonna Need It), we defer this overhead until the time of need. Our toolset helps make this more efficient, as we'll see in Chapter 3.

Figure 2-3 shows a data pipeline to calculate the number of emails sent between two email addresses.

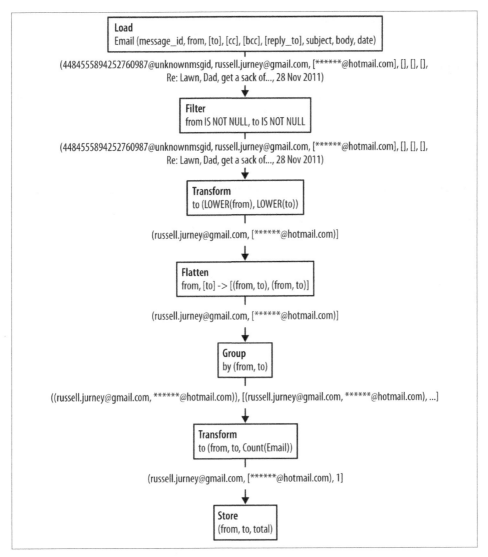

Figure 2-3. Simple dataflow to count the number of emails sent between two email addresses

While this dataflow may look complex now if you're used to SQL, you'll quickly get used to working this way and such a simple flow will become second nature.

Data Perspectives

To start, it is helpful to highlight different ways of looking at email. In Agile Big Data, we employ varied perspectives to inspect and mine data in multiple ways because it is easy to get stuck thinking about data in one or two ways that you find productive. Next, we'll discuss the different perspectives on email data we'll be using throughout the book.

Networks

A social network is a group of persons (egos) and the connections or links between them. These connections may be directed, as in "Bob knows Sara." Or they may be undirected: "Bob and Sara are friends." Connections may also have a connection strength, or weight. "Bob knows Sara well," (on a scale of 0 to 1) or "Bob and Sara are married" (on a scale of 0 to 1).

The sender and recipients of an email via the *from*, *to*, *cc*, and *bcc* fields can be used to create a social network. For instance, this email defines two entities, `russell.ju rney@gmail.com` and `******@hotmail.com`.

```
From: Russell Jurney <russell.jurney@gmail.com>
To: ******* Jurney <******@hotmail.com>
```

The message itself implies a link between them. We can represent this as a simple social network, as shown in Figure 2-4.

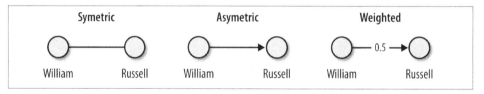

Figure 2-4. Social network dyad

Figure 2-5 depicts a more complex social network.

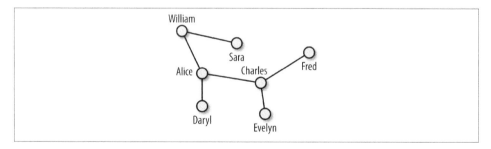

Figure 2-5. Social network

Figure 2-6 shows a social network of some 200 megabytes of emails from Enron.

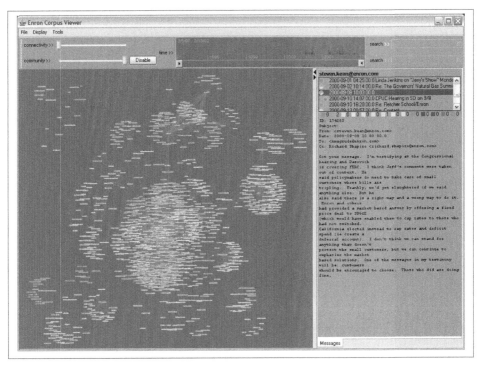

Figure 2-6. Enron corpus viewer, by Jeffrey Heer and Andrew Fiore

Social network analysis, or SNA, is the scientific study and analysis of social networks. By modeling our inbox as a social network, we can draw on the methods of SNA (like PageRank) to reach a deeper understanding of the data and of our interpersonal network. Figure 2-7 shows such an analysis applied to the Enron network.

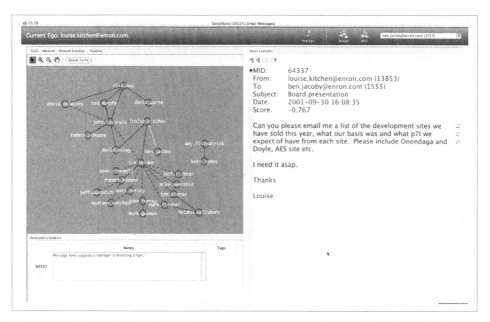

Figure 2-7. Enron SocialRank, by Jaime Montemayor, Chris Diehl, Mike Pekala, and David Patrone

Time Series

A time series is a sequence of data points ordered by a timestamp recorded with each value. Time series allow us to see changes and trends in data over time. All emails have timestamps, so we can represent a series of emails as a time series, as Figure 2-8 demonstrates.

```
Date: Mon, 28 Nov 2011 14:57:38 -0800
```

Looking at several other emails, we can plot the raw data in a time series.

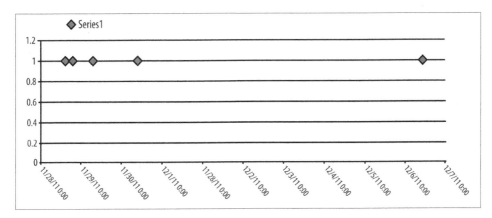

Figure 2-8. Raw time series

Since we aren't looking at another value associated with the time series, we can see the data more clearly by bucketing it by day (see Figure 2-9). This will tell us how many emails were sent between these two addresses per day.

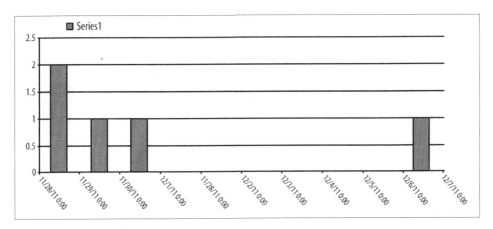

Figure 2-9. Grouped time series

Time series analysis might tell us when we most often receive email from a particular person or even what that person's work schedule is.

Natural Language

The meat of an email is its text content. Despite the addition of MIME for multimedia attachments, email is still primarily text.

```
Subject: Re: Lawn
Content-Type: text/plain; charset=ISO-8859-1
```

```
Dad, get a sack of Rye grass seed and plant it over there now.  It
will build up a nice turf over the winter, then die off when it warms
up.  Making for good topsoil you can plant regular grass in.

Will keep the weeds from taking over.

Russell Jurney
twitter.com/rjurney
russell.jurney@gmail.com
datasyndrome.com
```

We might analyze the body of the email by counting its word frequency. Once we remove noncoding common stopwords (like *of* and *it*), this looks like Figure 2-10.

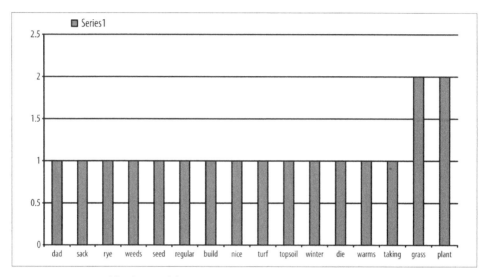

Figure 2-10. Email body word frequency

We might use this word frequency to infer that the topics of the email are *plant* and *grass*, as these are the most common words. Processing natural language in this way helps us to extract properties from semistructured data to make it more structured. This enables us to incorporate these structured properties into our analysis.

A fun way to show word frequency is via a *wordle*, illustrated in Figure 2-11.

Figure 2-11. Email body wordle

Probability

In probability theory, we model seemingly random processes by counting the occurrence and co-occurence of different properties in our data to create probability distributions. We can then employ these probability distributions to make suggestions and to classify entities into different categories.

We can use probability distributions to make predictions. For instance, we might create a probability distribution for our sent emails using the *from, to,* and *cc* fields. Given that our email address, *russell.jurney@gmail.com,* appears in the *from* field, and another email address appears in the *to* field, what is the chance that another email will appear *cc*'d?

In this case, our raw data is the *to, from,* and *cc* fields from each email:

```
From: Russell Jurney <russell.jurney@gmail.com>
To: ****** Jurney <******@hotmail.com>
Cc: Ruth Jurney <****@hotmail.com>
```

First, we count the pairs of *from* email addresses with *to* email addresses. This is called the *co-occurrence* of these two properties. Let's highlight one pair in particular, those emails between O'Reilly editor Mike Loukides and me (Table 2-1).

Table 2-1. Totals for to, from pairs

From	To	Count
russell.jurney@gmail.com	****.jurney@gmail.com	10
russell.jurney@gmail.com	toolsreq@oreilly.com	10
russell.jurney@gmail.com	yoga*****@gmail.com	11
russell.jurney@gmail.com	user@pig.apache.org	14
russell.jurney@gmail.com	*****@hotmail.com	15
russell.jurney@gmail.com	**mikel@oreilly.com**	**28**
russell.jurney@gmail.com	russell.jurney@gmail.com	44

Dividing these values by the total number of emails gives us a probability distribution characterizing the odds that any given email from our email address will be to any given email (Table 2-2).

Table 2-2. P(to|from): probability of to, given from

From	To	Probability
russell.jurney@gmail.com	****.jurney@gmail.com	0.0359
russell.jurney@gmail.com	toolsreq@oreilly.com	0.0359
russell.jurney@gmail.com	yoga*****@gmail.com	0.0395
russell.jurney@gmail.com	user@pig.apache.org	0.0503
russell.jurney@gmail.com	*****@hotmail.com	0.0539
russell.jurney@gmail.com	**mikel@oreilly.com**	**0.1007**
russell.jurney@gmail.com	russell.jurney@gmail.com	0.1582

Finally, we list the probabilities for a pair recipients co-occurring, given that the first address appears in an email (Table 2-3).

Table 2-3. P(cc|from ∩ to): probability of cc, given from and to

From	To	Cc	Probability
russell.jurney@gmail.com	**mikel@oreilly.com**	**toolsreq@oreilly.com**	**0.0357**
russell.jurney@gmail.com	**mikel@oreilly.com**	**meghan@oreilly.com**	**0.25**
russell.jurney@gmail.com	**mikel@oreilly.com**	**mstallone@oreilly.com**	**0.25**
russell.jurney@gmail.com	toolsreq@oreilly.com	meghan@oreilly.com	0.1
russell.jurney@gmail.com	toolsreq@oreilly.com	mikel@oreilly.com	0.2

We can then use this data to show who else is likely to appear in an email, given a single address. This data can be used to drive features like Gmail's suggested recipients feature, as shown in Figure 2-12.

Figure 2-12. Gmail suggested recipients

We'll see later how we can use Bayesian inference to make reasonable suggestions for recipients, even when Table 2-3 is incomplete.

Conclusion

As we've seen, viewing semistructured data according to different algorithms, structures, and perspectives informs feature development more than normalizing and viewing it in structured tables does. We'll be using the perspectives defined in this chapter to create features throughout the book, as we climb the data-value pyramid. In the next chapter, you'll learn how to specify schemas in our analytic stores using Apache Pig directly.

## CHAPTER 3

Agile Tools

This chapter will briefly introduce our software stack. This stack is optimized for our process. By the end of this chapter, you'll be collecting, storing, processing, publishing, and decorating data. Our stack enables one person to do all of this, to go "full stack." We'll cover a lot, and quickly, but don't worry: I will continue to demonstrate this software stack in Chapters 5 through 10. You need only understand the basics now; you will get more comfortable later.

We begin with instructions for running our stack in local mode on your own machine. In the next chapter, you'll learn how to scale this same stack in the cloud via Amazon Web Services. Let's get started.

Code examples for this chapter are available at *https://github.com/rjurney/ Agile_Data_Code/tree/master/ch03*. Clone the repository and follow along!

```
git clone https://github.com/rujrney/Agile_Data_Code.git
```

Scalability = Simplicity

As NoSQL tools like Hadoop, MongoDB, data science, and big data have developed, much focus has been placed on the plumbing of analytics applications. This book teaches you to build applications that use such infrastructure. We will take this plumbing for granted and build applications that depend on it. Thus, this book devotes only two chapters to infrastructure: one on introducing our development tools, and the other on scaling them up in the cloud to match our data's scale.

In choosing our tools, we seek linear scalability, but above all, we seek simplicity. While the concurrent systems required to drive a modern analytics application at any kind of scale are complex, we still need to be able to focus on the task at hand: processing data to create value for the user. When our tools are too complex, we start to focus on the tools themselves, and not on our data, our users, and new applications to help them.

An effective stack enables collaboration by teams that include diverse sets of skills such as design and application development, statistics, machine learning, and distributed systems.

 The stack outlined in this book is not definitive. It has been selected as an example of the kind of end-to-end setup you should expect as a developer or should aim for as a platform engineer in order to rapidly and effectively build analytics applications. The takeaway should be an example stack you can use to jumpstart your application, and a standard to which you should hold other stacks.

Agile Big Data Processing

The first step to building analytics applications is to plumb your application from end to end: from collecting raw data to displaying something on the user's screen (see Figure 3-1). This is important, because complexity can increase fast, and you need user feedback plugged into the process from the start, lest you start iterating without feedback (also known as the *death spiral*).

Figure 3-1. Flow of data processing in Agile Big Data

The components of our stack are thus:

- **Events** are the things logs represent. An event is an occurrence that happens and is logged along with its features and timestamps.

  Events come in many forms—logs from servers, sensors, financial transactions, or actions our users take in our own application. To facilitate data exchange among different tools and languages, events are serialized in a common, agreed-upon format.

- **Collectors** are event aggregators. They collect events from numerous sources and log them in aggregate to bulk storage, or queue them for action by sub-real-time workers.

- **Bulk storage** is a filesystem capable of parallel access by many concurrent processes. We'll be using S3 in place of the Hadoop Distributed FileSystem (HDFS) for this purpose. HDFS sets the standard for bulk storage, and without it, big data would not exist. There would be no cheap place to store vast amounts of data where it can be accessed with high I/O throughput for the kind of processing we do in Agile Big Data.

- **Distributed document stores** are multinode stores using document format. In Agile Big Data, we use them to publish data for consumption by web applications and other services. We'll be using MongoDB as our distributed document store.

- A minimalist web **application server** enables us to plumb our data as JSON through to the client for visualization, with minimal overhead. We use Python/Flask. Other examples are Ruby/Sinatra or Node.js.

- A modern **browser** or mobile application enables us to present our data as an interactive experience for our users, who provide data through interaction and events describing those actions. In this book, we focus on web applications.

This list may look daunting, but in practice, these tools are easy to set up and match the crunch points in data science. This setup scales easily and is optimized for analytic processing.

Setting Up a Virtual Environment for Python

In this book, we use Python 2.7, which may or may not be the version you normally use. For this reason, we'll be using a virtual environment (*http://www.virtualenv.org/en/ latest/index.html*) (venv). To set up venv, install the virtualenv package.

With pip:

```
pip install virtualenv
```

With easy_install:

```
easy_install virtualenv
```

I have already created a venv environment in GitHub. Activate it via:

```
source venv/bin/activate
```

If, for some reason, the included venv does not work, then set up your virtual environment as follows:

```
virtualenv -p `which python2.7` venv --distribute
source venv/bin/activate
```

Now you can run `pip install -r requirements.txt` to install all required packages, and they will build under the *venv/* directory.

To exit your virtual environment:

```
deactivate
```

Serializing Events with Avro

In our stack, we use a serialization system called Avro (see Figure 3-2). Avro allows us to access our data in a common format across languages and tools.

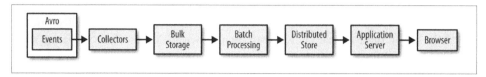

Figure 3-2. Serializing events

Avro for Python

Installation

To install Avro for Python, you must first build and install the snappy compression library, available at *http://code.google.com/p/snappy/*. Using a package manager to do so is recommended. Then install python-snappy via easy_install, pip, or from the source at *https://github.com/andrix/python-snappy*. With python-snappy installed, Avro for Python should install without problems.

To install the Python Avro client from source:

```
[bash]$ git clone https://github.com/apache/avro.git
[bash]$ cd avro/lang/py
[bash]$ python setup.py install
```

To install using pip or easy_install:

```
pip install avro
```

```
easy_install avro
```

Testing

Try writing and reading a simple schema to verify that our data works (see Example 3-1):

```
[bash]$ python
```

Example 3-1. Writing avros in python (ch03/python/test_avro.py)

```
# Derived from the helpful example at
http://www.harshj.com/2010/04/25/writing-and-reading-avro-data-files-using-python/
from avro import schema, datafile, io
import pprint
OUTFILE_NAME = '/tmp/messages.avro'
SCHEMA_STR = """{
    "type": "record",
    "name": "Message",
    "fields" : [
      {"name": "message_id", "type": "int"},
```

```
        {"name": "topic", "type": "string"},
        {"name": "user_id", "type": "int"}
    ]
}"""
SCHEMA = schema.parse(SCHEMA_STR)
# Create a 'record' (datum) writer
rec_writer = io.DatumWriter(SCHEMA)

# Create a 'data file' (avro file) writer
df_writer = datafile.DataFileWriter(
  open(OUTFILE_NAME, 'wb'),
  rec_writer,
  writers_schema = SCHEMA
)

df_writer.append( {"message_id": 11, "topic": "Hello galaxy", "user_id": 1} )
df_writer.append( {"message_id": 12, "topic": "Jim is silly!", "user_id": 1} )
df_writer.append( {"message_id": 23, "topic": "I like apples.", "user_id": 2} )
df_writer.close()
```

Verify that the messages are present:

```
[bash]$ ls -lah /tmp/messages.avro

-rw-r--r--  1 rjurney  wheel   263B Jan 23 17:30 /tmp/messages.avro
```

Now verify that we can read records back (Example 3-2).

Example 3-2. Reading avros in Python (ch03/python/test_avro.py)

```
from avro import schema, datafile, io
import pprint
# Test reading avros
rec_reader = io.DatumReader()

# Create a 'data file' (avro file) reader
df_reader = datafile.DataFileReader(
  open(OUTFILE_NAME),
  rec_reader
)

# Read all records stored inside
pp = pprint.PrettyPrinter()
for record in df_reader:
  pp.pprint(record)
```

The output should look like this:

```
{u'message_id': 11, u'topic': u'Hello galaxy', u'user_id': 1}
{u'message_id': 12, u'topic': u'Jim is silly!', u'user_id': 1}
{u'message_id': 23, u'topic': u'I like apples.', u'user_id': 2}
```

Collecting Data

We'll be collecting your own email via IMAP, as shown in Figure 3-3, and storing it to disk with Avro (Figure 3-3). Email conforms to a well-known schema defined in RFC-2822. We'll use a simple utility to encapsulate the complexity of this operation. If an error or a slow Internet connection prevents you from downloading your entire inbox, that's OK. You only need a few megabytes of data to work the examples, although more data makes the examples richer and more rewarding.

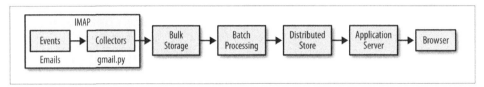

Figure 3-3. Collecting data via IMAP

Example 3-3. Avro schema for email (ch03/gmail/email.avro.schema)

```
{
        "type":"record",
        "name":"Email",
        "fields":[
           { "name":"message_id", "type":["null","string"] },
           { "name":"thread_id",   "type":["null","string"] },
           { "name":"in_reply_to","type":["string","null"] },
           { "name":"subject",     "type":["string","null"] },
           { "name":"body",        "type":["string","null"] },
           { "name":"date",        "type":["string","null"] },
           {
              "name":"from",
              "type":
              {
                "type":"record","name":"from",
                "fields":[
                   { "name":"real_name", "type":["null","string"] },
                   { "name":"address",   "type":["null","string"] }
              ] }
           },
           {
              "name":"tos",
              "type":[
                "null",
                {
                   "type":"array",
                   "items":[
                     "null",
                     {
                        "type":"record","name":"to",
```

```json
                            "fields":[
                                { "name":"real_name", "type":["null","string"] },
                                { "name":"address",    "type":["null","string"] }
            ] } ] } ]
        },
        {
            "name":"ccs",
            "type":[
                "null",
                {
                    "type":"array",
                    "items":[
                        "null",
                        {
                            "type":"record","name":"cc",
                            "fields":[
                                { "name":"real_name", "type":["null","string"] },
                                { "name":"address",    "type":["null","string"] }
            ] } ] } ]
        },
        {
            "name":"bccs",
            "type":[
                "null",
                {
                    "type":"array",
                    "items":[
                        "null",
                        {
                            "type":"record","name":"bcc",
                            "fields":[
                                { "name":"real_name", "type":["null","string"] },
                                { "name":"address",    "type":["null","string"] }
            ] } ] } ]
        },
        {
            "name":"reply_tos",
            "type":[
                "null",
                {
                    "type":"array",
                    "items":[
                        "null",
                        {
                            "type":"record","name":"reply_to",
                            "fields":[
                                { "name":"real_name", "type":["null","string"] },
                                { "name":"address",    "type":["null","string"] }
            ] } ] } ] }
    ]
}
```

Python's imaplib makes connecting to Gmail easy, as shown in Example 3-4.

Example 3-4. Scraping IMAP with gmail.py

```
def init_imap(username, password, folder):
  imap = imaplib.IMAP4_SSL('imap.gmail.com', 993)
  imap.login(username, password)
  status, count = imap.select(folder)
  return imap, count
```

With this in place, and a helper script, we can scrape our own inbox like so using *gmail.py*:

```
Usage: gmail.py -m <mode: interactive|automatic>
-u <username@gmail.com>
-p <password>
-s <schema_path>
-f <imap_folder>
-o <output_path>
```

We should use automatic mode for collecting our emails. Email subjects will print to the screen as they download. This can take a while if you want the entire inbox, so it is best to leave it to download overnight.

You can stop the download at any time with Control-C to move on.

```
[jira] [Commented] (PIG-2489) Input Path Globbing{} not working with
PigStorageSchema or PigStorage('\t', '-schema');
[jira] [Created] (PIG-2489) Input Path Globbing{} not working with
PigStorageSchema or PigStorage('\t', '-schema');
Re: hbase dns lookups
Re: need help in rendering treemap
RE: HBase 0.92.0 is available for download
Prescriptions Ready at Walgreens
Your payment to AT&T MOBILITY has been sent
Prometheus Un Bound commented on your status.
Re: HBase 0.92.0 is available for download
Prescriptions Ready at Walgreens
How Logical Plan Generator works?
Re: server-side SVG-based d3 graph generation, and SVG display on IE8
neil kodner (@neilkod) favorited one of your Tweets!
```

Now that we've got data, we can begin processing it.

Data Processing with Pig

> Perl is the duct tape of the Internet.
>
> —Hassan Schroeder, Sun's first webmaster

Pig is the duct tape of big data. We use it to define dataflows in Hadoop so that we can pipe data between best-of-breed tools and languages in a structured, coherent way. Because Pig is a client-side technology, you can run it on local data, against a Hadoop cluster, or via Amazon's Elastic MapReduce (EMR). This enables us to work locally and at scale with the same tools. Figure 3-4 shows Pig in action.

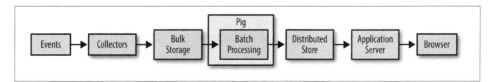

Figure 3-4. Processing data with Pig

Installing Pig

At the time of writing, Pig 0.11 is the latest version. Check here to see if there is a newer version, and if so, use it instead: *http://pig.apache.org/releases.html*.

To install Pig on your local machine, follow the Getting Started directions at *http://pig.apache.org/docs/r0.11.0/start.html*.

```
cd /me
wget http://apache.osuosl.org/pig/pig-0.11.1/pig-0.11.1.tar.gz
tar -xvzf pig-0.11.1.tar.gz
cd pig-0.11.1
ant
cd contrib/piggybank/java
ant
cd
echo 'export PATH=$PATH:/me/pig-0.11.1/bin' >> ~/.bash_profile
source ~/.bash_profile
```

Now test Pig on the emails from your inbox we stored as avros. Run Pig in local mode (instead of Hadoop mode) via -x `local` and put logfiles in */tmp* via -l `/tmp` to keep from cluttering your workspace.

```
cd pig; pig -l /tmp -x local -v -w sent_counts.pig
```

Our Pig script, *ch03/pig/sent_counts.pig*, flows our data through filters to clean it, and then projects, groups, and counts it to determine sent counts (Example 3-5).

Example 3-5. Processing data with Pig

```
/* Set Home Directory - where we install software */
%default HOME `echo \$HOME/Software/`

REGISTER $HOME/pig/build/ivy/lib/Pig/avro-1.5.3.jar
REGISTER $HOME/pig/build/ivy/lib/Pig/json-simple-1.1.jar
REGISTER $HOME/pig/contrib/piggybank/java/piggybank.jar

DEFINE AvroStorage org.apache.pig.piggybank.storage.avro.AvroStorage();
```

```
rmf /tmp/sent_counts.txt

/* Load the emails in avro format (edit the path to match where you saved them)
using the AvroStorage UDF from Piggybank */
messages = LOAD '/me/Data/test_mbox' USING AvroStorage();

/* Filter nulls, they won't help */
messages = FILTER messages BY (from IS NOT NULL) AND (tos IS NOT NULL);

/* Emails can be 'to' more than one person. FLATTEN() will project our from with
each 'to' that exists. */addresses = FOREACH messages GENERATE from.address AS
from, FLATTEN(tos.(address)) AS to;

/* Lowercase the email addresses, so we don't count MiXed case of the same address
as multiple addresses */lowers = FOREACH addresses GENERATE LOWER(from) AS from,
LOWER(to) AS to;

/* GROUP BY each from/to pair into a bag (array), then count the bag's contents
($1 means the 2nd field) to get a total.
   Same as SQL: SELECT from, to, COUNT(*) FROM lowers GROUP BY (from, to);
   Note: COUNT_STAR differs from COUNT in that it counts nulls. */
by_from_to = GROUP lowers BY (from, to);
sent_counts = FOREACH by_from_to GENERATE FLATTEN(group) AS (from, to),
   COUNT_STAR(lowers) AS total;

/* Sort the data, highest sent count first */
sent_counts = ORDER sent_counts BY total DESC;
STORE sent_counts INTO '/tmp/sent_counts.txt';
```

Since we stored without specifying a storage function, Pig uses PigStorage. By default, PigStorage produces tab-separated values. We can simply cat the file, or open it in Excel (as shown in Figure 3-5).

```
cat /tmp/sent_counts.txt/part-*

    erictranslates@gmail.com d3-js@googlegroups.com 1
    info@meetup.com russell.jurney@gmail.com 1
    jira@apache.org pig-dev@hadoop.apache.org 1
    desert_rose_170@hotmail.com user@hbase.apache.org 1
    fnickels@gmail.com d3-js@googlegroups.com 1
    l.garulli@gmail.com gremlin-users@googlegroups.com 1
    punk.kish@gmail.com d3-js@googlegroups.com 1
    lists@ruby-forum.com user@jruby.codehaus.org 1
    rdm@cfcl.com ruby-99@meetup.com 1
    sampd@stumbleupon.com user@pig.apache.org 1
    sampd@stumbleupon.com user@hive.apache.org 1
    kate.jurney@gmail.com russell.jurney@gmail.com 2
    bob@novus.com d3-js@googlegroups.com 2
    dalia.mohsobhy@hotmail.com user@hbase.apache.org 2
    hugh.lomas@lodestarbpm.com d3-js@googlegroups.com 2
    update+mkd57whm@facebookmail.com russell.jurney@gmail.com 2
    notification+mkd57whm@facebookmail.com 138456936208061@groups.facebook.com 3
```

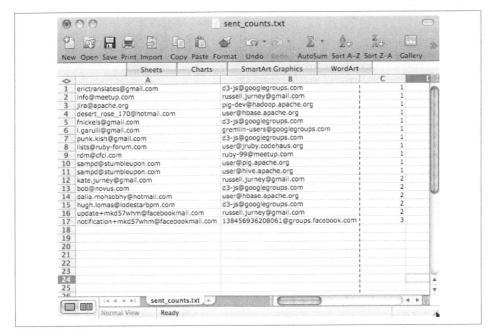

Figure 3-5. Pig output in Excel

You can see how the data flows in Figure 3-6. Each line of a Pig Latin script specifies some transformation on the data, and these transformations are executed stepwise as data flows through the script.

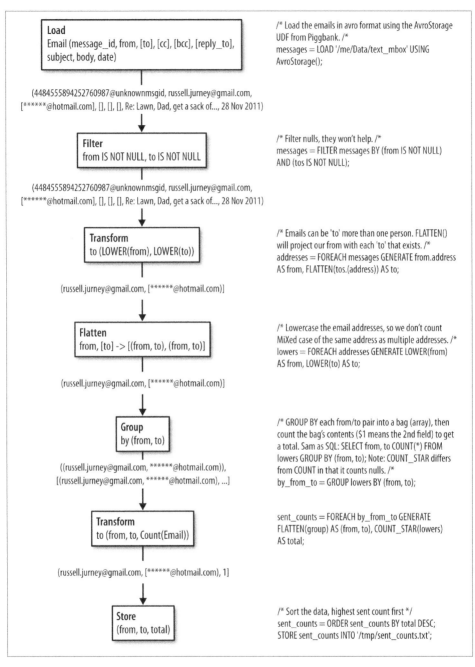

Load
Email (message_id, from, [to], [cc], [bcc], [reply_to], subject, body, date)

/* Load the emails in avro format using the AvroStorage UDF from Piggbank. /*
messages = LOAD '/me/Data/text_mbox' USING AvroStorage();

(4484555894252760987@unknownmsgid, russell.jurney@gmail.com, [*****@hotmail.com], [], [], [], Re: Lawn, Dad, get a sack of..., 28 Nov 2011)

Filter
from IS NOT NULL, to IS NOT NULL

/* Filter nulls, they won't help. /*
messages = FILTER messages BY (from IS NOT NULL) AND (tos IS NOT NULL);

(4484555894252760987@unknownmsgid, russell.jurney@gmail.com, [*****@hotmail.com], [], [], [], Re: Lawn, Dad, get a sack of..., 28 Nov 2011)

Transform
to (LOWER(from), LOWER(to))

/* Emails can be 'to' more than one person. FLATTEN() will project our from with each 'to' that exists. /*
addresses = FOREACH messages GENERATE from.address AS from, FLATTEN(tos.(address)) AS to;

(russell.jurney@gmail.com, [*****@hotmail.com])

Flatten
from, [to] -> [(from, to), (from, to)]

/* Lowercase the email addresses, so we don't count MiXed case of the same address as multiple addresses. /*
lowers = FOREACH addresses GENERATE LOWER(from) AS from, LOWER(to) AS to;

(russell.jurney@gmail.com, [*****@hotmail.com])

Group
by (from, to)

/* GROUP BY each from/to pair into a bag (array), then count the bag's contents ($1 means the 2nd field) to get a total. Sam as SQL: SELECT from, to COUNT(*) FROM lowers GROUP BY (from, to); Note: COUNT_STAR differs from COUNT in that it counts nulls. /*
by_from_to = GROUP lowers BY (from, to);

((russell.jurney@gmail.com, *****@hotmail.com)), [(russell.jurney@gmail.com, *****@hotmail.com), ...]

Transform
to (from, to, Count(Email))

sent_counts = FOREACH by_from_to GENERATE FLATTEN(group) AS (from, to), COUNT_STAR(lowers) AS total;

(russell.jurney@gmail.com, [*****@hotmail.com), 1]

Store
(from, to, total)

/* Sort the data, highest sent count first */
sent_counts = ORDER sent_counts BY total DESC;
STORE sent_counts INTO '/tmp/sent_counts.txt';

Figure 3-6. Dataflow through a Pig Latin script

Publishing Data with MongoDB

To feed our data to a web application, we need to publish it in some kind of database. While many choices are appropriate, we'll use MongoDB for its ease of use, document orientation, and excellent Hadoop and Pig integration (Figure 3-7). With MongoDB and Pig, we can define any arbitrary schema in Pig, and mongo-hadoop (*https://github.com/mongodb/mongo-hadoop*) will create a corresponding schema in MongoDB. There is no overhead in managing schemas as we derive new relations—we simply manipulate our data into publishable form in Pig. That's agile!

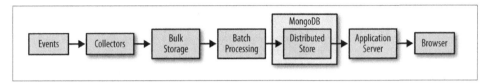

Figure 3-7. Publishing data to MongoDB

Installing MongoDB

Excellent instructions for installing MongoDB are available at *http://www.mongodb.org/display/DOCS/Quickstart*. An excellent tutorial is available here: *http://www.mongodb.org/display/DOCS/Tutorial*. I recommend completing these brief tutorials before moving on.

Download MongoDB for your operating system at *http://www.mongodb.org/downloads*.

```
cd /me
wget http://fastdl.mongodb.org/osx/mongodb-osx-x86_64-2.0.2.tgz
tar -xvzf mongodb-osx-x86_64-2.0.2.tgz
sudo mkdir -p /data/db/
sudo chown `id -u` /data/db
```

Now start the MongoDB server:

```
cd /me/mongodb-osx-x86_64-2.0.2
bin/mongodb 2>&1 &
```

Now open the mongo shell, and get help:

```
bin/mongo
> help
```

Finally, create our collection and insert and query a record:

```
> use agile_data
> e = {from: 'russell.jurney@gmail.com', to: 'bumper1700@hotmail.com',
subject: 'Grass seed', body: 'Put grass on the lawn...'}
> db.email.save(e)
```

```
> db.email.find()
{ "_id" : ObjectId("4f21c5f7c6ef8a98a43d921b"), "from" :
"russell.jurney@gmail.com",
"to" : "bumper1700@hotmail.com", "subject" : "Grass seed",
"body" : "Put grass on the lawn..." }
```

We're cooking with Mongo! We'll revisit this operation later.

Installing MongoDB's Java Driver

MongoDB's Java driver is available at *https://github.com/mongodb/mongo-java-driver/ downloads*. At the time of writing, the 2.10.1 version is the latest stable build: *https:// github.com/downloads/mongodb/mongo-java-driver/mongo-2.10.1.jar*.

```
wget https://github.com/downloads/mongodb/mongo-java-driver/mongo-2.10.1.jar
mv mongo-2.10.1.jar /me/mongo-hadoop/
```

Installing mongo-hadoop

Once we have the Java driver to MongoDB, we're ready to integrate with Hadoop. MongoDB's Hadoop integration is available at *https://github.com/mongodb/mongo-hadoop* and can be downloaded at *https://github.com/mongodb/mongo-hadoop/tarball/master* as a *tar/gzip* file.

```
cd /me
git clone git@github.com:rjurney/mongo-hadoop.git
cd mongo-hadoop
sbt package
```

Pushing Data to MongoDB from Pig

Pushing data to MongoDB from Pig is easy.

First we'll run *ch03/pig/mongo.pig* to store the sent counts we computed to MongoDB, as shown in Example 3-6.

Example 3-6. Pig to MongoDB (ch03/pig/mongo.pig)

```
REGISTER $HOME/mongo-hadoop/mongo-2.10.1.jar
REGISTER $HOME/mongo-hadoop/core/target/mongo-hadoop-core-1.1.0-SNAPSHOT.jar
REGISTER $HOME/mongo-hadoop/pig/target/mongo-hadoop-pig-1.1.0-SNAPSHOT.jar

set mapred.map.tasks.speculative.execution false
set mapred.reduce.tasks.speculative.execution false

sent_counts = LOAD '/tmp/sent_counts.txt' AS (from:chararray, to:chararray, total:long);
STORE sent_counts INTO 'mongodb://localhost/agile_data.sent_counts' USING
com.mongodb.hadoop.pig.MongoStorage();
```

Now we'll query our data in Mongo!

```
use agile_data

> db.sent_counts.find()
  { "from" : "erictranslates@gmail.com", "to" : "d3-js@googlegroups.com",
    "total" : 1 }
  { "from" : "info@meetup.com", "to" : "russell.jurney@gmail.com",
    "total" : 1 }
  { "from" : "jira@apache.org", "to" : "pig-dev@hadoop.apache.org",
    "total" : 1 }
  { "from" : "desert_rose_170@hotmail.com", "to" : "user@hbase.apache.org",
    "total" : 1 }
  { "from" : "fnickels@gmail.com", "to" : "d3-js@googlegroups.com",
    "total" : 1 }
  { "from" : "l.garulli@gmail.com", "to" : "gremlin-users@googlegroups.com",
    "total" : 1 }
  { "from" : "punk.kish@gmail.com", "to" : "d3-js@googlegroups.com",
    "total" : 1 }
  { "from" : "lists@ruby-forum.com", "to" : "user@jruby.codehaus.org",
    "total" : 1 }
  { "from" : "rdm@cfcl.com", "to" : "ruby-99@meetup.com", "total" : 1 }
  { "from" : "sampd@stumbleupon.com", "to" : "user@pig.apache.org",
    "total" : 1 }
  { "from" : "sampd@stumbleupon.com", "to" : "user@hive.apache.org",
    "total" : 1 }
  { "from" : "kate.jurney@gmail.com", "to" : "russell.jurney@gmail.com",
    "total" : 2 }
  { "from" : "bob@novus.com", "to" : "d3-js@googlegroups.com",
    "total" : 2 }
  { "from" : "dalia.mohsobhy@hotmail.com", "to" : "user@hbase.apache.org",
    "total" : 2 }
  { "from" : "hugh.lomas@lodestarbpm.com", "to" : "d3-js@googlegroups.com",
    "total" : 2 }
  { "from" : "update+mkd57whm@facebookmail.com", "to" : "russell.jurney@gmail.com",
    "total" : 2 }
  { "from" : "notification+mkd57whm@facebookmail.com", "to" :
    "138456936208061@groups.facebook.com", "total" : 3 }

> db.sent_counts.find({from: 'kate.jurney@gmail.com', to:
    'russell.jurney@gmail.com'})
  { "from" : "kate.jurney@gmail.com", "to" : "russell.jurney@gmail.com",
    "total" : 2 }
```

Congratulations, you've published Agile Big Data! Note how easy that was: once we had our data prepared, it is a one-liner to publish it with Mongo! There is no schema overhead, which is what we need for how we work. We don't know the schema until we're ready to store, and when we do, there is little use in specifying it externally to our Pig code. This is but one part of the stack, but this property helps us work rapidly and enables agility.

Speculative Execution and Hadoop Integration

We haven't set any indexes in MongoDB, so it is possible for copies of entries to be written. To avoid this, we must turn off speculative execution in our Pig script.

```
set mapred.map.tasks.speculative.execution false
```

Hadoop uses a feature called *speculative execution* to fight *skew*, the bane of concurrent systems. Skew is when one part of the data, assigned to some part of the system for processing, takes much longer than the rest of the data. Perhaps there are 10,000 entries for all keys in your data, but one has 1,000,000. That key can end up taking much longer to process than the others. To combat this, Hadoop runs a race—multiple mappers or reducers will process the lagging chunk of data. The first one wins!

This is fine when writing to the Hadoop filesystem, but this is less so when writing to a database without primary keys that will happily accept duplicates. So we turn this feature off in Example 3-6, via set mapred.map.tasks.speculative.execution false.

Searching Data with ElasticSearch

ElasticSearch (*http://www.elasticsearch.org/*) is emerging as "Hadoop for search," in that it provides a robust, easy-to-use search solution that lowers the barrier of entry to individuals wanting to search their data, large or small. ElasticSearch has a simple RESTful JSON interface, so we can use it from the command line or from any language. We'll be using ElasticSearch to search our data, to make it easy to find the records we'll be working so hard to create.

Installation

Excellent tutorials on ElasticSearch are available at *http://www.elasticsearchtutorial.com/elasticsearch-in-5-minutes.html* and *https://github.com/elasticsearch/elasticsearch#getting-started*.

ElasticSearch is available for download at *http://www.elasticsearch.org/download/*.

```
wget https://github.com/downloads/elasticsearch/elasticsearch/
    elasticsearch-0.20.2.tar.gz
tar -xvzf elasticsearch-0.20.2.tar.gz
cd elasticsearch-0.20.2
mkdir plugins
bin/elasticsearch -f
```

That's it! Our local search engine is up and running!

ElasticSearch and Pig with Wonderdog

Infochimps' (*http://www.infochimps.com/*) Wonderdog (*https://github.com/ infochimps-labs/wonderdog*) provides integration between Hadoop, Pig, and Elastic-Search. With Wonderdog, we can load and store data from Pig to and from our search engine. This is extremely powerful, because it lets us plug a search engine into the end of our data pipelines.

Installing Wonderdog

You can download Wonderdog here: *https://github.com/infochimps-labs/wonderdog.*

```
git clone https://github.com/infochimps-labs/wonderdog.git
mvn install
```

Wonderdog and Pig

To use Wonderdog with Pig, load the required jars and run *ch03/pig/elasticsearch.pig.*

```
/* Avro uses json-simple, and is in piggybank until Pig 0.12, where AvroStorage
and TrevniStorage are builtins */
REGISTER $HOME/pig/build/ivy/lib/Pig/avro-1.5.3.jar
REGISTER $HOME/pig/build/ivy/lib/Pig/json-simple-1.1.jar
REGISTER $HOME/pig/contrib/piggybank/java/piggybank.jar

DEFINE AvroStorage org.apache.pig.piggybank.storage.avro.AvroStorage();

/* Elasticsearch's own jars */
REGISTER $HOME/elasticsearch-0.20.2/lib/*.jar

/* Register wonderdog - elasticsearch integration */
REGISTER $HOME/wonderdog/target/wonderdog-1.0-SNAPSHOT.jar

/* Remove the old json */
rmf /tmp/sent_count_json

/* Nuke the elasticsearch sent_counts index, as we are about to replace it. */
sh curl -XDELETE 'http://localhost:9200/inbox/sent_counts'

/* Load Avros, and store as JSON */
sent_counts = LOAD '/tmp/sent_counts.txt' AS (from:chararray, to:chararray,
total:long);
STORE sent_counts INTO '/tmp/sent_count_json' USING JsonStorage();

/* Now load the JSON as a single chararray field, and index it into ElasticSearch
with Wonderdog from InfoChimps */
sent_count_json = LOAD '/tmp/sent_count_json' AS (sent_counts:chararray);
STORE sent_count_json INTO 'es://inbox/sentcounts?json=true&size=1000' USING
com.infochimps.elasticsearch.pig.ElasticSearchStorage(
  '$HOME/elasticsearch-0.20.2/config/elasticsearch.yml',
  '$HOME/elasticsearch-0.20.2/plugins');

/* Search for Hadoop to make sure we get a hit in our sent_count index */
```

```
sh curl -XGET 'http://localhost:9200/inbox/sentcounts/_search?q=russ&pretty=
true&size=1'
```

Searching our data

Now, searching our data is easy, using curl:

```
curl -XGET 'http://localhost:9200/sent_counts/sent_counts/_search?q=
russell&pretty=true'
```

```
{
  "took" : 4,
  "timed_out" : false,
  "_shards" : {
    "total" : 5,
    "successful" : 5,
    "failed" : 0
  },
  "hits" : {
    "total" : 13,
    "max_score" : 1.2463257,
    "hits" : [ {
      "_index" : "inbox",
      "_type" : "sentcounts",
      "_id" : "PmiMqM51SUi3L4-Xr9iDTw",
      "_score" : 1.2463257, "_source" : {"to":"russell@getnotion.com","total":1,
"from":"josh@getnotion.com"}
    }, {
      "_index" : "inbox",
      "_type" : "sentcounts",
      "_id" : "iog-R1OoRYO32oZX-W1DUw",
      "_score" : 1.2463257, "_source" : {"to":"russell@getnotion.com","total":7,"
from":"mko@getnotion.com"}
    }, {
      "_index" : "inbox",
      "_type" : "sentcounts",
      "_id" : "Y1VA0MX8TOW35sPuw3ZEtw",
      "_score" : 1.2441664, "_source" : {"to":"russell@getnotion.com","total":1,
"from":"getnotion@jiveon.com"}
    } ]
  }
}
```

Clients for ElasticSearch for many languages are available at *http://www.elastic search.org/guide/appendix/clients.html.*

Python and ElasticSearch with pyelasticsearch

For Python, pyelasticsearch (*http://pyelasticsearch.readthedocs.org/en/ latest/*) is a good choice. To make it work, we'll first need to install the Python Requests (*http://bit.ly/18Lt29u*) library.

Using pyelasticsearch is easy: run *ch03/pig/elasticsearch.pig.*

```
import pyelasticsearch
elastic = pyelasticsearch.ElasticSearch('http://localhost:9200/inbox')
results = elastic.search("hadoop", index="sentcounts")
print results['hits']['hits'][0:3]

[
    {
        u'_score': 1.0898509,
        u'_type': u'sentcounts',
        u'_id': u'FFGklMbtTdehUxwezlLS-g',
        u'_source': {
            u'to': u'hadoop-studio-users@lists.sourceforge.net',
            u'total': 196,
            u'from': u'hadoop-studio-users-request@lists.sourceforge.net'
        },
        u'_index': u'inbox'
    },
    {
        u'_score': 1.084789,
        u'_type': u'sentcounts',
        u'_id': u'rjxnV1zST62XoP6IQV25SA',
        u'_source': {
            u'to': u'user@hadoop.apache.org',
            u'total': 2,
            u'from': u'hadoop@gmx.com'
        },
        u'_index': u'inbox'
    },
    {
        u'_score': 1.084789,
        u'_type': u'sentcounts',
        u'_id': u'dlIdbCPjRcSOLiBZkshIkA',
        u'_source': {
            u'to': u'hadoop@gmx.com',
            u'total': 1,
            u'from': u'billgraham@gmail.com'
        },
        u'_index': u'inbox'
    }
]
```

Reflecting on our Workflow

Compared to querying MySQL or MongoDB directly, this workflow might seem hard.
Notice, however, that our stack has been optimized for time-consuming and thoughtful
data processing, with occasional publishing. Also, this way we won't hit a wall when our
real-time queries don't scale anymore as they becoming increasingly complex.

Once our application is plumbed efficiently, the team can work together efficiently, but
not before. The stack is the foundation of our agility.

Lightweight Web Applications

The next step is turning our published data into an interactive application. As shown in Figure 3-8, we'll use lightweight web frameworks to do that.

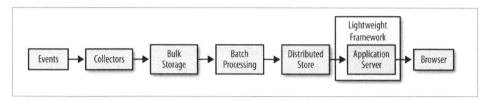

Figure 3-8. To the Web with Python and Flask

We choose lightweight web frameworks because they are simple and fast to work with. Unlike CRUD applications, mined data is the star of the show here. We use read-only databases and simple application frameworks because that fits with the applications we build and how we offer value.

Given the following examples in Python/Flask, you can easily implement a solution in Sinatra, Rails, Django, Node.js, or your favorite language and web framework.

Python and Flask

According to the Bottle Documentation (*http://bottlepy.org/docs/dev/*), "Flask is a fast, simple, and lightweight WSGI micro web framework for Python."

Excellent instructions for using Flask are available at *http://flask.pocoo.org/*.

Flask Echo ch03/python/flask_echo.py

Run our echo Flask app, *ch03/python/flask_echo.py*.

```
from flask import Flask
app = Flask(__name__)

@app.route("/<input>")
def hello(input):
  return input

if __name__ == "__main__":
  app.run(debug=True)

$ curl http://localhost:5000/hello%20world!

hello world!
```

Python and Mongo with pymongo

Pymongo presents a simple interface for MongoDB in Python. To test it out, run *ch03/python/flask_echo.py*.

```
import pymongo
import json

conn = pymongo.Connection() # defaults to localhost
db = conn.agile_data
results = db['sent_counts'].find()
for i in range(0, results.count()): # Loop and print all results
  print results[i]
```

The output is like so:

```
{u'total': 22994L, u'to': u'pig-dev@hadoop.apache.org', u'_id': ObjectId
('50ea5e0a30040697fb0f0710'), u'from': u'jira@apache.org'}
{u'total': 3313L, u'to': u'russell.jurney@gmail.com', u'_id': ObjectId
('50ea5e0a30040697fb0f0711'), u'from': u'twitter-dm-russell.jurney=
  gmail.com@postmaster.twitter.com'}
{u'total': 2406L, u'to': u'russell.jurney@gmail.com', u'_id': ObjectId
('50ea5e0a30040697fb0f0712'), u'from': u'notification+mkd57whm@facebookmail.com'}
{u'total': 2353L, u'to': u'russell.jurney@gmail.com', u'_id': ObjectId
('50ea5e0a30040697fb0f0713'), u'from': u'twitter-follow-russell.jurney=
  gmail.com@postmaster.twitter.com'}
```

Displaying sent_counts in Flask

Now we use pymongo with Flask to display the *sent_counts* we stored in Mongo using Pig and MongoStorage. Run *ch03/python/flask_mongo.py*.

```
from flask import Flask
import pymongo
import json

# Set up Flask
app = Flask(__name__)

# Set up Mongo
conn = pymongo.Connection() # defaults to localhost
db = conn.agile_data
sent_counts = db['sent_counts']

# Fetch from/to totals, given a pair of email addresses
@app.route("/sent_counts/<from_address>/<to_address>")
def sent_count(from_address, to_address):
  sent_count = sent_counts.find_one( {'from': from_address, 'to': to_address} )
  return json.dumps( {'from': sent_count['from'], 'to': sent_count['to'], 'total'
: sent_count['total']} )

if __name__ == "__main__":
  app.run(debug=True)
```

Now visit a URL you know will contain records from your own inbox (for me, this is *http://localhost:5000/sent_counts/russell.jurney@gmail.com/*******@gmail.com*) and you will see:

```
{"ego1":"russell.jurney@gmail.com","ego2":"*******@gmail.com","total":8}
```

And we're done! (See Figure 3-9).

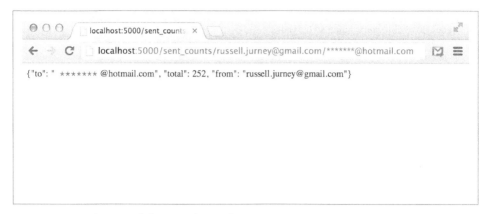

Figure 3-9. Undecorated data on the Web

Congratulations! You've published data on the Web. Now let's make it presentable.

Presenting Our Data

Design and presentation impact the value of your work. In fact, one way to think of Agile Big Data is as data design. The output of our data models matches our views, and in that sense design and data processing are not distinct. Instead, they are part of the same collaborative activity: data design. With that in mind, it is best that we start out with a solid, clean design for our data and work from there (see Figure 3-10).

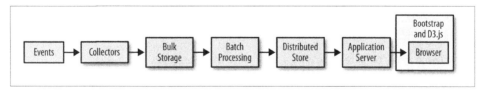

Figure 3-10. Presenting our data with Bootstrap and D3.js and nvd3.js

Installing Bootstrap

According to the Bootstrap Project (*http://twitter.github.com/bootstrap*):

Bootstrap is Twitter's toolkit for kickstarting CSS for websites, apps, and more. It includes base CSS styles for typography, forms, buttons, tables, grids, navigation, alerts, and more.

Bootstrap is available at *http://twitter.github.com/bootstrap/assets/bootstrap.zip*. To install, place it with the static files of your application and load it in an HTML template.

```
wget http://twitter.github.com/bootstrap/assets/bootstrap.zip
unzip bootstrap.zip
```

We've already installed Bootstrap at *ch03/web/static/bootstrap*.

To invoke Bootstrap, simply reference it as CSS from within your HTML page—for example, from *ch03/web/templates/table.html*.

```
<link href="/static/bootstrap/css/bootstrap.css" rel="stylesheet">
```

Booting Boostrap

It takes only a little editing of an example to arrive at a home page for our project, as shown in Figure 3-11.

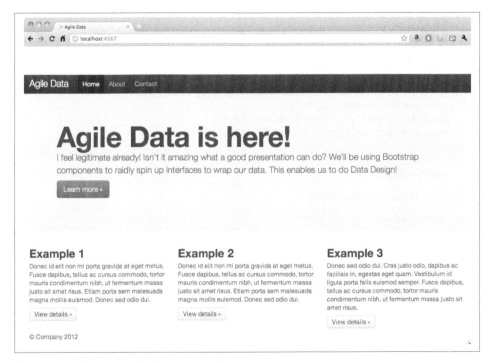

Figure 3-11. Bootstrap 2.0 hero example

Let's try wrapping a previous example in a table, styled with Bootstrap.

That's right: tables for tabular data! Bootstrap lets us use them without shame. Now we'll update our controller to stash our data, and create a simple template to print a table.

In *index.py*:

```python
from flask import Flask, render_template
import pymongo
import json
import re

# Set up Flask
app = Flask(__name__)

# Set up Mongo
conn = pymongo.Connection() # defaults to localhost
db = conn.agile_data

# Fetch from/to totals and list them
@app.route("/sent_counts")
def sent_counts():
  sent_counts = db['sent_counts'].find()
  results = {}
  results['keys'] = 'from', 'to', 'total'
  results['values'] = [[s['from'], s['to'], s['total']]
    for s in sent_counts if re.search('apache', s['from']) or
      re.search('apache', s['to'])]
  results['values'] = results['values'][0:17]
  return render_template('table.html', results=results)

if __name__ == "__main__":
  app.run(debug=True)
```

And in our template, *table.html*:

```html
<!DOCTYPE html>
<html lang="en">
  <head>
    <meta charset="utf-8">
    <title>Agile Big Data - Inbox Explorer</title>
    <!-- Derived from example at http://twitter.github.com/bootstrap/
      examples/sticky-footer.html -->
    <meta name="viewport" content="width=device-width, initial-scale=1.0">
    <meta name="description" content="">
    <meta name="author" content="Russell Jurney">

    <!-- CSS -->
    <link href="/static/bootstrap/css/bootstrap.css" rel="stylesheet">
    <style type="text/css">

      /* Sticky footer styles
```

```
------------------------------------------------ */

html,
body {
  height: 100%;
  /* The html and body elements cannot have any padding or margin. */
}

/* Wrapper for page content to push down footer */
#wrap {
  min-height: 100%;
  height: auto !important;
  height: 100%;
  /* Negative indent footer by it's height */
  margin: 0 auto -60px;
}

/* Set the fixed height of the footer here */
#push,
#footer {
  height: 60px;
}
#footer {
  background-color: #f5f5f5;
}

/* Lastly, apply responsive CSS fixes as necessary */
@media (max-width: 767px) {
  #footer {
    margin-left: -20px;
    margin-right: -20px;
    padding-left: 20px;
    padding-right: 20px;
  }
}

/* Custom page CSS
------------------------------------------------ */
/* Not required for template or sticky footer method. */

.container {
  width: auto;
  max-width: 1000px;
}
.container .credit {
  margin: 20px 0;
}

.container[role="main"] {
    padding-bottom: 60px;
}
```

```
    #footer {
        position: fixed;
        bottom: 0;
        left: 0;
        right: 0;
    }

    .lead { margin-top: -15px; }

  </style>
  <link href="/static/bootstrap/css/bootstrap-responsive.css" rel="stylesheet">

  <!-- HTML5 shim, for IE6-8 support of HTML5 elements -->
  <!--[if lt IE 9]>
    <script src="http://html5shim.googlecode.com/svn/trunk/html5.js"></script>
  <![endif]-->
</head>

<body>

  <!-- Part 1: Wrap all page content here -->
  <div id="wrap">

    <!-- Begin page content -->
    <div class="container">
      <div class="page-header">
        <h1>Analytic Inbox</h1>
      </div>
      <p class="lead">Email Sent Counts</p>
      <table class="table table-striped table-bordered table-condensed">
        <thead>
          {% for key in results['keys'] -%}
            <th>{{ key }}</th>
          {% endfor -%}
        </thead>
        <tbody>
          {% for row in results['values'] -%}
          <tr>
            {% for value in row -%}
            <td>{{value}}</td>
            {% endfor -%}
          </tr>
          {% endfor -%}
        </tbody>
      </table>
    </div>

    <div id="push"></div>
  </div>

  <div id="footer">
    <div class="container">
```

```
<!-- <p class="muted credit">Example courtesy <a href="http://martinbean.
    co.uk">Martin Bean</a> and <a href="http://ryanfait.com/sticky-
    footer/">Ryan Fait</a>.</p> -->
<p class="muted credit"><a href="http://shop.oreilly.com/product/
    0636920025054.do">Agile Big Data</a> by <a href="http://
    www.linkedin.com/in/russelljurney">Russell Jurney</a>, 2013
</div>
</div>
<!-- Le javascript
================================================== -->
<!-- Placed at the end of the document so the pages load faster -->
<script src="../assets/js/jquery.js"></script>
<script src="/static/bootstrap/js/bootstrap.min.js"></script>
</body>
</html>
```

The result, shown in Figure 3-12, is human-readable data with very little trouble!

Figure 3-12. Simple data in a Bootstrap-styled table

In practice, we may use client-side templating languages like mous-
tache (*http://mustache.github.com/*). For clarity's sake, we use Jinja2
templates in this book.

Visualizing Data with D3.js and nvd3.js

D3.js (*http://d3js.org/*) enables data-driven documents. According to its creator, Mike
Bostock:

> d3 is not a traditional visualization framework. Rather than provide a monolithic system
> with all the features anyone may ever need, d3 solves only the crux of the problem: efficient
> manipulation of documents based on data. This gives d3 extraordinary flexibility, ex-
> posing the full capabilities of underlying technologies such as CSS3, HTML5, and SVG.

We'll be using D3.js to create charts in our application. Like Bootstrap, it is already
installed in */static*.

```
wget d3js.org/d3.v3.zip
```

We'll be making charts with D3.js and nvd3.js later on. For now, take a look at the examples directory to see what is possible with D3.js: *https://github.com/mbostock/d3/wiki/Gallery* and *http://nvd3.org/ghpages/examples.html*.

Conclusion

We've created a very simple app with a single, very simple feature. This is a great starting point, but so what?

What's important about the application isn't what it does, but rather that it's a pipeline where it's easy to modify every stage. This is a pipeline that will scale without our worrying about optimization at each step, and where optimization becomes a function of cost in terms of resource efficiency, but not in terms of the cost of reengineering.

As we'll see in the next chapter, because we've created an arbitrarily scalable pipeline where every stage is easily modifiable, it is possible to return to agility. We won't quickly hit a wall as soon as we need to switch from a relational database to something else that "scales better," and we aren't subjecting ourselves to the limitations imposed by tools designed for other tasks like online transaction processing (Figure 3-13).

We now have total freedom to use best-of-breed tools within this framework to solve hard problems and produce value. We can choose any language, any framework, and any library and glue it together to get things built.

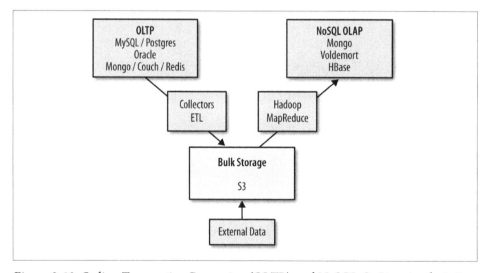

Figure 3-13. Online Transaction Processing (OLTP) and NoSQL OnLine Analytic Processing (OLAP)

## CHAPTER 4

To the Cloud!

The trend toward server-side computing and the exploding popularity of Internet services has created a new class of computing systems that we have named warehouse-scale computers, or WSCs. The name is meant to call attention to the most distinguishing feature of these machines: the massive scale of their software infrastructure, data repositories, and hardware platform. This perspective is a departure from a view of the computing problem that implicitly assumes a model where one program runs in a single machine. In warehouse-scale computing, the program is an Internet service, which may consist of tens or more individual programs that interact to implement complex end-user services such as email, search, or maps.

—Luiz André Barroso and Urs Hölzle,
The Datacenter as a Computer: An Introduction to the Design of Warehouse-Scale Machines (Morgan and Claypool)

Introduction

In this chapter, we will extend the stack we introduced in Chapter 3 into a scaled-up cloud stack (Figure 4-1 and Figure 4-2). In so doing, we will enable a bridge between local operations on sample data and those in the cloud at scale on big data. We'll be taking advantage of the cloud's elasticity along the way. In the following pages, we'll be employing such services as GitHub, dotCloud, and Amazon Web Services to deploy our application at scale. Doing so will allow us to proceed unencumbered by the limited resources of our own machines, and will enable access to vast resources and data.

Figure 4-1. The cloud

Cloud computing has revolutionized the development of new applications—greenfield projects unconstrained by existing infrastructure. For a new project, or a new company, cloud computing offers instant-on infrastructure that can scale with any load or any problem. More than that—once we accept that we must build horizontally scalable systems out of commodity components—cloud computing offers application development at the level of the composition of vast system components.

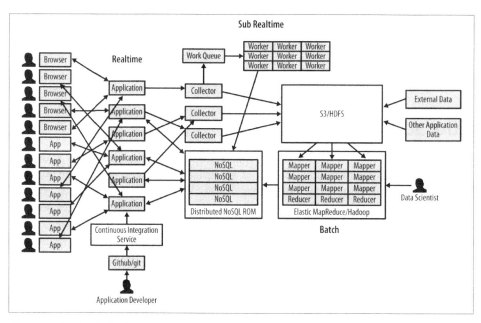

Figure 4-2. The Agile Big Data stack

We are able to operate in terms of systems in a datacenter controlled by a small team, composed into architecture on the fly and scaled up and down to match any load. In cloud computing, there is freedom to operate at new degrees of complexity via higher levels of abstraction and automation.

 Indeed, the development of cloud computing is as fundamental as electrification, whereby clock cycles replace electrons, and we are only beginning to see the consequences of its potential. As research scientist and author Andrew McAfee writes in his blog post "The Cloudy Future of Corporate IT (*http://bit.ly/1dUxd61*)": "The real impact of the new technology was not apparent right away. Electrical power didn't just save costs or make factories a bit more efficient. It allowed radically new designs and approaches."

Code examples for this chapter are available at *https://github.com/rjurney/ Agile_Data_Code/tree/master/ch04*. Clone the repository and follow along!

```
git clone https://github.com/rjurney/Agile_Data_Code.git
```

GitHub

Git is a fast, distributed version control system created by Linus Torvalds for the Linux Kernel. Git addresses the operational problems large projects had with there being a single serial "repository of record."

In providing a concurrent source code repository, Git enabled the creation of the social network GitHub (*http://github.com*), which enables collaboration and monitoring of myriad software projects and their authors. GitHub has become a jumping-off point for other web services, and we will use it to deploy our application to the cloud.

Excellent instructions for getting started with GitHub are available at *http:// help.github.com/*, so we will not repeat them here. Sign up for a GitHub basic account if you do not already have one.

dotCloud

dotCloud, shown in Figure 4-3, is a cloud application platform. Sitting on top of Amazon Web Services, it abstracts away the complexity of building reliable web application and database hosting, while still being accessible to other Amazon Web Services. Higher-level tools and platforms are more powerful, and we will be using dotCloud in place of building our own high-availability web server and MongoDB clusters.

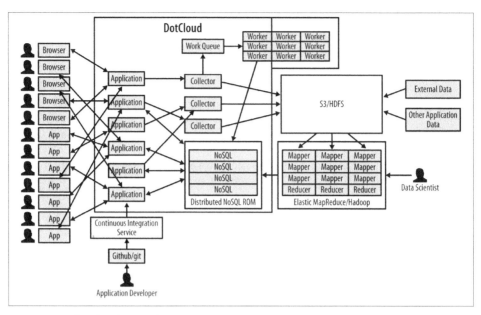

Figure 4-3. dotCloud in Agile Big Data

Although there are other "cloud platform as a service" providers, we'll use dotCloud because it supports many languages, offers Amazon Web Services interoperability, autoscales in response to load, and includes a rich library of services for databases and other features.

Echo on dotCloud

Excellent instructions for getting started with dotCloud and Python are available at *http://docs.dotcloud.com/0.9/firststeps/install/* and *http://docs.dotcloud.com/0.9/serv ices/python/*, so we will not repeat them here. Set up a dotCloud account if you do not already have one, and create a dotCloud project pointing at the GitHub project *ch04* you set up in the last section.

The initial application code for our project is simple, as you can see in Example 4-1.

Example 4-1. app.py

```
#!/usr/bin/env python2.7

from flask import Flask
import os

# Set up Flask
app = Flask(__name__)

# Simple echo service
```

```
@app.route("/<string:input>")
def hello(input):
  return input

if __name__ == "__main__":
  port = int(os.environ.get('PORT', 5000))
  app.run(host='0.0.0.0', port=port)
```

Edit *ch04/dotcloud.yml* to specify our application's resources: a Python application with system dependencies (Ubuntu packages), and a MongoDB database instance.

```
www:
  type: python
  systempackages:
    - libatlas-base-dev
    - gfortran
    - libsnappy1
    - libsnappy-dev
data:
  type: mongodb
```

Finally, edit *ch04/wsgi.py*, which shows dotCloud how to run your web application, as shown in Example 4-2.

Example 4-2. wsgi.py

```
import sys
sys.path.append('/home/dotcloud/current')
from index import app as application
```

Now ensure the dotCloud CLI is installed on your machine: *http://docs.dotcloud.com/0.9/firststeps/install/*.

That's it. We can now create a dotCloud application with `dotcloud create myapp`, and update/deploy the application with `dotcloud push`. For this minor trouble, we get a highly available application server that can autoscale with the push of a button.

Use `dotcloud setup` to configure your environment:

```
dotcloud setup
<dotCloud username or email: russell.jurney@gmail.com
Password:
==> dotCloud authentication is complete! You are recommended to run `dotcloud
check` now.
```

`dotcloud create` will set up an application like so:

```
$ dotcloud create testola
==> Creating a sandbox application named "testola"
==> Application "testola" created.
Connect the current directory to "testola"? [Y/n]: y
==> Connecting with the application "testola"
==> Connected with default push options: --rsync
```

To update code, run dotcloud push:

```
...
02:29:15.262548: [www] Build completed successfully. Compiled image size is 38MB
02:29:15.279736: [www] Build successful for service (www)
02:29:15.290683: --> Application (testola) build is done
02:29:15.311308: --> Provisioning services' instances... (This may take a bit)
02:29:15.338441: [www] Using default scaling for service www (1 instance(s)).
02:29:15.401420: [www.0] Provisioning service (www) instance #0
02:29:16.414451: [data] Using default scaling for service data (1 instance(s)).
02:29:16.479846: [data.0] Provisioning service (data) instance #0
02:30:00.606768: --> All service instances have been provisioned. Installing...
02:30:00.685336: [www.0] Installing build revision rsync-136003975113 for service
                        (www) instance #0
02:30:22.430300: [www.0] Running postinstall script...
02:30:23.745193: [www.0] Launching...
02:30:28.173168: [www.0] Waiting for the instance to become responsive...
02:30:41.201260: [www.0] Re-routing traffic to the new build...
02:30:43.199746: [www.0] Successfully installed build revision rsync-
                        1360203975113 for service (www) instance #0
02:30:43.208778: [www.0] Installation successful for service (www) instance #0
02:30:43.211030: --> Application (testola) fully installed
==> Application is live at http://testola-rjurney.dotcloud.com
```

To monitor logs, use dotcloud logs.

Our server is up at the URL given, in this case *http://testola-rjurney.dotcloud.com*. Visiting our app with some input, *http://testola-rjurney.dotcloud.com/hello world* shows us our application is running, as shown in Figure 4-4.

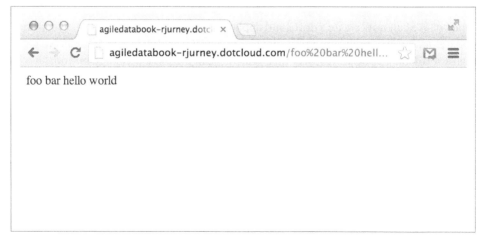

Figure 4-4. dotCloud echo service

We can now use Git to release our application continuously as we mine and publish new data to display.

Python Workers

dotCloud provides Python workers that can help process events of content that is generated on the fly, and that takes longer than a web request to process, but not so long that we would want to wait for an entire Hadoop job to finish. Instructions on using Python dotCloud workers can be found at *http://docs.dotcloud.com/0.9/services/python-worker/*.

Amazon Web Services

According to the whitepaper "Building Fault-Tolerant Applications on AWS (*http://bit.ly/19TmHaZ*)":

> Amazon Web Services (AWS) provides a platform that is ideally suited for building fault-tolerant software systems. However, this attribute is not unique to our platform. Given enough resources and time, one can build a fault-tolerant software system on almost any platform. The AWS platform is unique because it enables you to build fault-tolerant systems that operate with a minimal amount of human interaction and up-front financial investment.

Amazon is the leading cloud provider, setting the standard against which others are measured. Amazon has managed to continue to innovate, rolling out many new offerings at higher and higher levels each year.

More important, dotCloud and the other platform-as-a-service (PaaS) offerings we are using are built on top of AWS. This allows us to use these platforms directly with AWS offerings like S3 and EC2. This means we can roll custom infrastructure when it is called for, and rely on platforms as a service to save time otherwise.

Simple Storage Service

Amazon's Simple Storage Service (S3) is a cloud-based replacement for the Hadoop filesystem: vast, distributed, reliable storage that can be read concurrently from many processes. S3 is highly available, and is well connected to other services.

S3 should be the dumping ground for all data associated with your project. All logs, scrapes, and database dumps go here. We will combine datasets on S3 to produce more value, then publish them to MongoDB.

Download the s3cmd utility (*http://s3tools.org/s3cmd*) from *http://sourceforge.net/projects/s3tools/files/* and use it to upload your emails to S3.

```
[bash]$ s3cmd --configure
```

Your settings should look like this:

```
New settings:
Access Key: <access_key_id>
Secret Key: <secret_key>
Encryption password:
Path to GPG program: None
Use HTTPS protocol: True
HTTP Proxy server name:
HTTP Proxy server port: 0
```

Now create a bucket for your emails and upload them, as shown in Example 4-3. The bucket name will need to be unique, so personalize it.

Example 4-3. Upload our emails to S3

```
[bash]$ s3cmd mb s3://rjurney.email.upload
Bucket 's3://rjurney.email.upload/' created

[bash]$ s3cmd put --recursive /me/tmp/inbox s3://rjurney.email.upload
/me/tmp/inbox/part-0-0.avro -> s3://rjurney.email.upload/inbox/part-0-0.avro
[part 1 of 4, 15MB]
 15728640 of 15728640    100% in   21s   725.65 kB/s  done
/me/tmp/inbox/part-0-0.avro -> s3://rjurney.email.upload/inbox/part-0-0.avro
[part 2 of 4, 15MB]
  2322432 of 15728640     14% in    4s   533.93 kB/s
```

Now we're ready to process our data in the cloud.

Elastic MapReduce

Amazon's Elastic MapReduce, or EMR, allows us to spin up a Hadoop cluster of any size we like, and to rent it hourly to process our data. When we are finished, we throw the cluster away. This gives us the agility to scale our data processing to whatever load we throw at it in a moment's notice.

To start, set up a new job flow as shown in Figure 4-5.

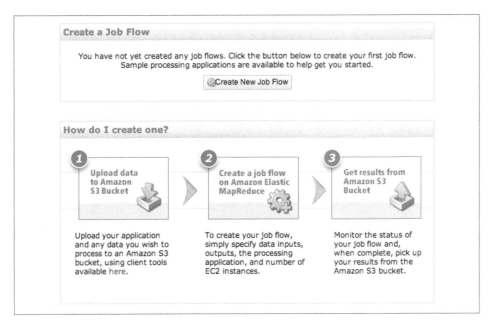

Figure 4-5. Elastic MapReduce: create a job flow

Select 'Run' your own application, and choose 'Pig Program' as the type (Figure 4-6). Then choose 'Start an Interactive Pig Session' (Figure 4-7). Finally, select a keypair for your session (Figure 4-8).

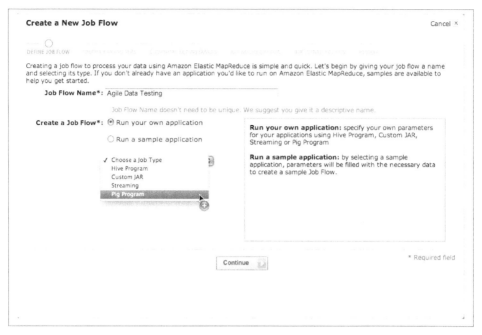

Figure 4-6. Elastic MapReduce: run a Pig program

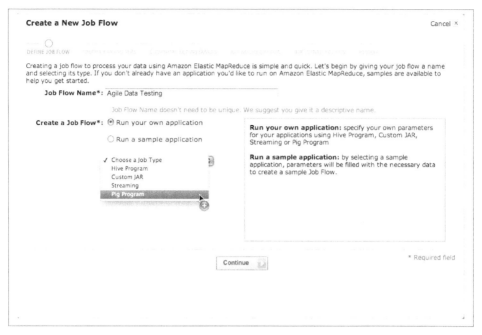

Figure 4-7. Elastic MapReduce: interactive Pig session

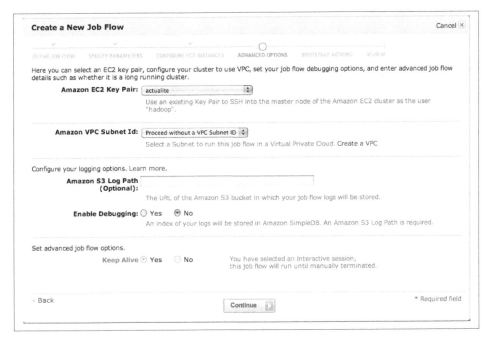

Figure 4-8. Elastic MapReduce: key selection

Select one small instance for the Hadoop master node, and five small instances for the core instance group (Figure 4-9). These five nodes will chew our emails in parallel, coordinated by the master node. The more nodes we add, the faster our data will be processed if we tell Pig to increase parallelism.

Figure 4-9. Elastic MapReduce: select instances

Launch this cluster, and then check the Elastic MapReduce section of the AWS console (Figure 4-10).

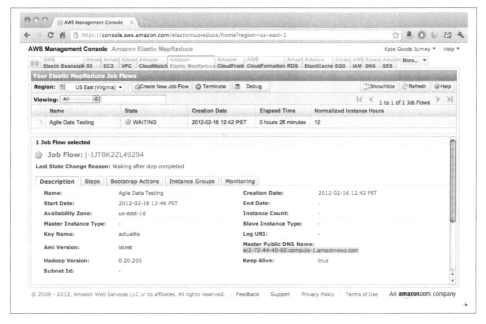

Figure 4-10. Elastic MapReduce console

Note the Master Public DNS Name. Once the cluster state shows the cluster is launched and ready, we can `ssh` to the name node and start our Pig session on our new Hadoop cluster. Remember to use the key with which we configured the cluster earlier.

```
ssh -i ~/.ssh/actualite.pem hadoop@ec2-given-ip.compute-1.amazonaws.com
```

You may now run Pig and proceed as you did in Chapter 3, substituting `s3n://` or `s3://` for `file://`.

Let's load the emails we uploaded previously and reexecute a Pig script—this time against five nodes.

```
REGISTER /me/pig/build/ivy/lib/Pig/avro-1.5.3.jar
REGISTER /me/pig/build/ivy/lib/Pig/json-simple-1.1.jar
REGISTER /me/pig/contrib/piggybank/java/piggybank.jar

/* This gives us a shortcut to call our Avro storage function */
DEFINE AvroStorage org.apache.pig.piggybank.storage.avro.AvroStorage();
rmf s3n://agile.data/sent_counts.txt

-- Load our emails using Pig's AvroStorage User Defined Function (UDF)
messages = LOAD 's3://agile.data/again_inbox' USING AvroStorage();

-- Filter missing from/to addresses to limit our processed data to valid records
messages = FILTER messages BY (from IS NOT NULL) AND (to IS NOT NULL);

-- Project all unique combinations of from/to in this message, then lowercase
```

```
emails  -- Note: Bug here if dupes with different case in one email.
smaller = FOREACH messages GENERATE FLATTEN(from) as from, FLATTEN(to) AS to;
pairs = FOREACH smaller GENERATE LOWER(from) AS from, LOWER(to) AS to;

-- Not group the data by unique pairs of addresses, take a count, and store as
   text in /tmp
froms = GROUP pairs BY (from, to) PARALLEL 10;
sent_counts = FOREACH froms GENERATE FLATTEN(group) AS (from, to), COUNT(pairs)
AS total; sent_counts = ORDER sent_counts BY total;

STORE sent_counts INTO 's3n://agile.data/sent_counts.txt';
```

We should see our successful job output, as shown in Figure 4-11.

```
...

Input(s):
Successfully read 55358 records (2636 bytes) from: "s3://agile.data/again_inbox"

Output(s):
Successfully stored 9467 records in: "s3n://agile.data/sent_counts.txt"
```

Note the parts in boldface. We are now loading and storing data via s3n URLs. We are also using the PARALLEL decorator to use multiple mappers and reducers on multiple nodes in parallel. As our data increases, so does the PARALLEL parameter. You can find out more about this parameter here: *http://pig.apache.org/docs/r0.9.2/cook book.html#Use+the+PARALLEL+Clause.*

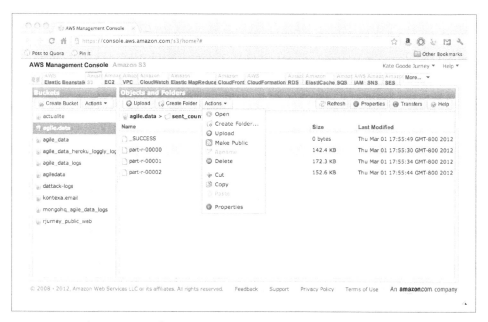

Figure 4-11. Elastic MapReduce actions

This script generates our `sent_counts` on S3, where they are accessible by any client with the right key. Note that S3 also allows us to publish this data directly—to one person or to everyone. It also allows us to push this content to the Cloudfront content distribution network. S3 gives us options. In Agile Big Data, we love options, as they enable innovation.

To learn more about Pig, read *Programming Pig* by Alan Gates (*http://oreil.ly/ 19fnO9W*) (O'Reilly).

Just like before on our local machine, what we really want to do is to easily publish our data to a database. That is where dotCloud's MongoDB resource comes in.

MongoDB as a Service

Much of the power of dotCloud is its rich library of services. We can use these services to avoid creating system components, outsourcing the complexity of configuring and operating these services without a loss of functionality. The only question, then, is reliability. Can we trust a relatively unknown database provider to keep up its service? What if there is data loss?

In Agile Big Data, we do not trust *any* database. All data we will be storing in MongoDB is derived and can be rederived and updated at any time. This lowers the bar considerably and allows us to take a chance on a new vendor in production when we might otherwise not.

At the time of writing, two EC2 MongoDB-as-a-service providers are available: MongoHQ and MongoLabs. Both are good choices, and both work with Elastic MapReduce. That being said, dotCloud has its own MongoDB service that we've provisioned under the `data` tag.

You can get info about the MongoDB instance we configured with the `dotcloud info data` command:

```
dotcloud info data
    == data
    type:              mongodb
    instances:         1
    reserved memory: N/A
    config:
      mongodb_nopreallocj:       True
      mongodb_oplog_size:        256
      mongodb_replset:           testola.data
      mongodb_password:          **************
      mongodb_logrotate_maxage:  30
      mongodb_noprealloc:        True
      mongodb_smallfiles:        True
    URLs:              N/A

    === data.0
```

```
datacenter:        Amazon-us-east-1d
service revision: mongodb/32d488a9ef44 (latest revision)
ports:
mongodb: mongodb://root:***@testola-rjurney-data-0.azva.dotcloud.net:40961
```

We'll use the MongoDB connection string in our Pig script to push data there. First we need to set up the `agile_data` database and user. To set up authentication, run `dotcloud run data mongo`.

```
use admin
db.auth("root", "*******");
```

Then, to set up our database, run:

```
use metrics
switched to db metrics
db.getSisterDB("admin").auth("root", "*******");
db.my_collection.save({"object": 1});
db.my_collection.count();
```

To set up a user, run:

```
use metrics
db.getSisterDB("admin").auth("root", "*******");
mynicedb.data:PRIMARY> db.addUser("jack", "OpenSesame");
```

Now our database is built, so let's use it to push data to Mongo!

Pushing data from Pig to MongoDB at dotCloud

Pushing data from Pig to dotCloud MongoDB works the same as before, but our connection string changes to the URI provided by dotCloud, with a new username and password plugged in (Example 4-4).

Example 4-4. Pig to dotCloud MongoDB

```
REGISTER /me/mongo-hadoop/mongo-2.7.3.jar
REGISTER /me/mongo-hadoop/core/target/mongo-hadoop-core-1.0.0-rc0.jar
REGISTER /me/mongo-hadoop/pig/target/mongo-hadoop-pig-1.0.0-rc0.jar

sent_counts = LOAD 's3://agile.data/sent_counts.txt' AS (from:chararray,
    to:chararray, total:int);
STORE sent_counts INTO
'mongodb://jack:OpenSesama@testola-rjurney-data-0.azva.dotcloud.net:40961/
  <agile_data>.sent_dist'
USING com.mongodb.hadoop.pig.MongoStorage;
```

Finally, we verify that our data is present in our new MongODB instance:

```
dotcloud run data mongo
==> Executing "mongo" on service (data) instance #0 (application testola)
^[[AMongoDB shell version: 2.2.2
connecting to: test

> use agile_data
```

```
> db.auth("jack", "OpenSesame")

> show collections
sent_dist
system.indexes
system.users

> db.sent_dist.find()
{ "_id" : ObjectId("4f41b927414e552992bf3911"), "from" : "k@123.org", "to" :
        "common-user@hadoop.apache.org", "total" : 3 }
{ "_id" : ObjectId("4f41b927414e552992bf3912"), "from" : "fm@hint.fm", "to" :
        "russell.jurney@gmail.com", "total" : 1 }
{ "_id" : ObjectId("4f41b927414e552992bf3913"), "from" : "li@idle.li", "to" :
        "user@hbase.apache.org", "total" : 3 }
...
```

That's it—we're publishing our data in the cloud!

Scaling MongoDB

We can scale MongoDB up at dotCloud by creating a replicated cluster, and by reading from the nonprimary nodes. dotCloud makes this easy with the Replica Set database type. The command is simple: `dotcloud scale data:instances=3`. More information on using replication is available at *http://www.mongodb.org/display/DOCS/Replica +Sets* and *http://docs.dotcloud.com/0.9/services/mongodb/#id1*. dotCloud also allows us to create dedicated clusters of up to five replicated EC2 nodes. We may not plan on using such capacity, but the fact that it is there with a few clicks makes dotCloud a great choice for our Agile Big Data stack.

To read from a secondary node, follow the directions here: *http://www.mongodb.org/ display/DOCS/Querying* on querying secondaries. Connect as normal and then run:

```
rs.slaveOk(); // enable querying a secondary
db.collection.find(...)
```

Instrumentation

If we aren't logging data on how our application is used, then we aren't able to run experiments that teach us about our users and how to meet their needs and give them value.

Google Analytics

Google Analytics (*http://www.google.com/analytics/*) provides basic capability to understand the traffic on your website. Sign up if you haven't already. Create a new property under the Admin>Accounts tab. Name it after your dotCloud site, in this case, *http://*

agiledatabook.dotcloud.com. Select, copy, and paste the tracking code into the *<head>* of your site-layout template like so:

```
<head>
    ...
    <script type="text/javascript">

    var _gaq = _gaq || [];
    _gaq.push(['_setAccount', 'XX-XXXXXXX-X']);
    _gaq.push(['_trackPageview']);

    (function() {
      var ga = document.createElement('script'); ga.type = 'text/javascript';
      ga.async = true;
      ga.src = ('https:' == document.location.protocol ? 'https://ssl' :
      'http://www') + '.google-analytics.com/ga.js';
      var s = document.getElementsByTagName('script')[0];
      s.parentNode.insertBefore(ga, s);
    })();

    </script>
</head>
```

That's it. We've inserted basic click tracking into our application.

Mortar Data

One way to accelerate Pig development is with the PaaS provider Mortar Data (Figure 4-12). Using Mortar Data, you can refine data in Pig and Python (as first-class user-defined functions [UDFs], including nltk, numpy, and scipy!), and publish to MongoDB—all from a clean, intuitive web interface.

Figure 4-12. Mortar Data

Climbing the Pyramid

If you can see your path laid out in front of you step by step, you know it's not your path. Your own path you make with every step you take. That's why it's your path.

—Joseph Campbell

Part II introduces the schema for the rest of the book: the data-value pyramid. Throughout the rest of our lessons, we will use the data-value pyramid to iteratively build value from very simple records up to interactive predictions. We begin with theory, then dive into practice using the framework I previously introduced.

Building Agile Big Data products means staging an environment where reproducible insights occur, are reinforced, and are extended up the value stack. It starts simply with displaying records. It ends with driving actions that create value and capture some of it. Along the way is a voyage of discovery.

The structure of this voyage, shown in Figure II.1, is called the data-value pyramid.

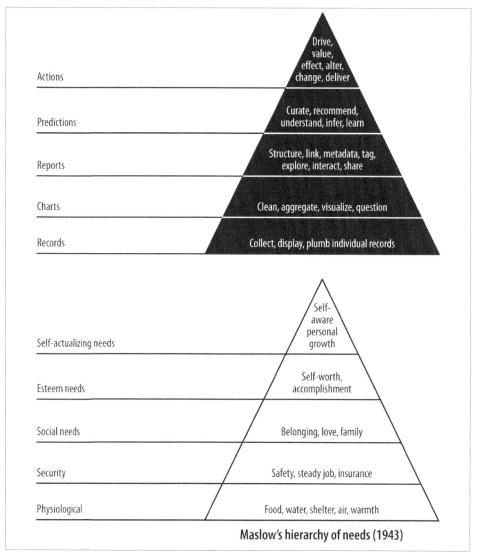

Figure II.1. The Jurney-Warden data-value pyramid of 2011

Climbing the Stack

The data-value stack mirrors Maslow's hierarchy of needs in the sense that lower levels must precede higher levels. The higher levels (like predictions) depend on the lower levels (like reports), so we can't skip steps. If we do so, we will lack sufficient structure and understanding of our data to easily build features and value at the higher levels.

The data-value stack begins with the simple display of records, where the focus is on connecting or "plumbing" our data pipeline all the way through from the raw data to the user's screen. We then move on to charts, where we extract enough structure from our data to display its properties in aggregate and start to familiarize ourselves with those properties. Next comes identifying relationships and exploring data through interactive reports. This enables statistical inference to generate predictions. Finally, we use these predictions to create value by driving user behavior and creating and capturing value.

To summarize, here are the components of the data-value stack:

Records
> The processing and display of atomic records through our entire stack

Charts
> Extracting properties from records in aggregate to produce charts

Reports
> Extracting relationships and trends to enable exploration and interactive charts

Predictions
> Using structure to make inferences, predictions, and recommendations

Actions
> Driving user behavior to create value and capture some of it

As we climb the stack, we extract increasing amounts of derived structure from our data to produce increasingly sophisticated features. Light is the best cleaner of data, and data that is not exposed in features seldom cleans itself. Structure and features are byproducts of each other. Therefore we cannot skip steps in the pyramid. Doing so undermines our ability to proceed further.

Nor can we specify features in later steps before working through those that precede them. Doing so results in lackluster products specified in the blind and uninformed by reality. We must respect that the data has its own opinion.

We'll be using this structure throughout the rest of the book to build our application around your email inbox.

Conclusion

The data-value pyramid enables agility by providing a structure for agile development cycles, helping to ensure that our development is broken up into short sprints. It serves as a conceptual framework to enable the kind of lightweight collaboration that characterizes agile efficiency.

## CHAPTER 5

Collecting and Displaying Records

In this chapter, our first agile sprint, we climb level 1 of the data-value pyramid (Figure 5-1). We will connect, or plumb, the parts of our data pipeline all the way through from raw data to a web application on a user's screen. This will enable a single developer to publish raw data records on the Web. In doing so, we will activate our stack against our real data, thereby connecting our application to the reality of our data and our users.

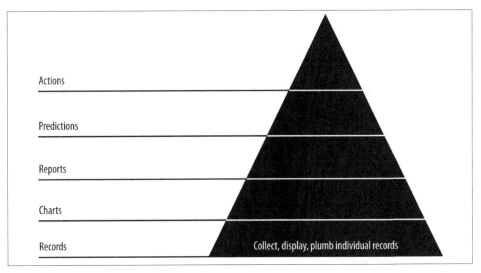

Actions

Predictions

Reports

Charts

Records   Collect, display, plumb individual records

Figure 5-1. Level 1: Displaying base records

If you already have a popular application, this step may seem confusing in that you already have the individual (or atomic) records displaying in your application. The point of this step, then, is to pipe these records through your analytical pipeline to bulk storage and then on to a browser. Bulk storage provides access for further processing via ETL (extract, transform, load) or some other means.

This setup and these records set the stage for further advances up the data-value pyramid as our complexity and value snowball.

 If your atomic records are petabytes, you may not want to publish them all to a document store. Moreover, security constraints may make this impossible. In that case, a sample will do. Prepare a sample and publish it, and then constrain the rest of your application as you create it.

Code examples for this chapter are available at *https://github.com/rjurney/ Agile_Data_Code/tree/master/ch05*. Clone the repository and follow along!

```
git clone https://github.com/rjurney/Agile_Data_Code.git
```

Putting It All Together

Setting up our stack was a bit of work. The good news is, with this stack, we don't have to repeat this work as soon as we start to see load from users on our system increase and our stack needs to scale. Instead, we'll be free to continue to iterate and improve our product from now on.

Now, let's work with some atomic records—our emails—to see how the stack works for us.

 An atomic record is a base record, the most granular of the events you will be analyzing. We might aggregate, count, slice, and dice atomic records, but they are indivisible. As such, they represent ground truth to us, and working with atomic records is essential to plugging into the reality of our data and our application.

Collect and Serialize Our Inbox

You can see the process of serializing events in Figure 5-2.

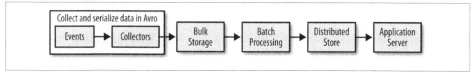

Figure 5-2. Serializing events

If you haven't already, download your Gmail inbox to Avro format. This can take a while to download, so you may need to let it run overnight.

 Store your emails to a location other than */tmp* to persist the data between reboots.

Download your inbox using *gmail.py*, as shown in Example 5-1.

Example 5-1. Collecting data: scrape our email inbox

```
Usage: gmail.py -m <mode: interactive|automatic> -u <username@gmail.com>
-p <password> -s <schema_path> -f <imap_folder> -o <output_path>
```

Our IMAP script is writing avros like this:

```
def process_email(self, raw_email, thread_id):
  avro_parts = dict({
    'message_id': self.strip_brackets(msg['Message-ID']),
    'thread_id': thread_id,
    'in_reply_to': self.strip_brackets(msg['In-Reply-To']),
    'subject': subject,
    'date': self.parse_date(msg['Date']),
    'body': body,
    'from': from_value,
    'tos': self.parse_addrs(msg['To']),
    'ccs': self.parse_addrs(msg['Cc']),
    'bccs': self.parse_addrs(msg['Bcc']),
    'reply_tos': self.parse_addrs(msg['Reply-To'])
  })
  return avro_parts, charset

  ...

  status, email_hash = fetch_email(imap, str(id))
  if(status == 'OK'):
  avro_writer.append(email_hash)
```

Here's an example command that will get the Gmail All Mail box:

```
./gmail.py -m automatic -u my.name@gmail.com -p '********' -s ./email.avro.schema
-f '[Gmail]/All Mail' -o /tmp/my_emails
```

Process and Publish Our Emails

Having collected our inbox data, let's process it (Figure 5-3). In the interest of plumbing our stack all the way through with real data to give us a base state to build from, let's publish the emails right away to MongoDB, so we can access them from Mongo and Flask.

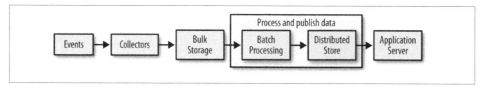

Figure 5-3. Processing and publishing data

Pig's MongoDB integration makes this easy. Look at *ch05/pig/avro_to_mongo.pig* (Example 5-2).

Example 5-2. Publishing emails to MongoDB

```
/* Set Home Directory - where we install software */
%default HOME `echo \$HOME/Software/`

/* Load Avro jars and define shortcut */
REGISTER $HOME/pig/build/ivy/lib/Pig/avro-1.5.3.jar
REGISTER $HOME/pig/build/ivy/lib/Pig/json-simple-1.1.jar
REGISTER $HOME/pig/contrib/piggybank/java/piggybank.jar
define AvroStorage org.apache.pig.piggybank.storage.avro.AvroStorage();

/* MongoDB libraries and configuration */
REGISTER $HOME/mongo-hadoop/mongo-2.10.1.jar
REGISTER $HOME/mongo-hadoop/core/target/mongo-hadoop-core-1.1.0-SNAPSHOT.jar
REGISTER $HOME/mongo-hadoop/pig/target/mongo-hadoop-pig-1.1.0-SNAPSHOT.jar

set mapred.map.tasks.speculative.execution false
set mapred.reduce.tasks.speculative.execution false

/* Set speculative execution off so we don't have the chance of duplicate
  records in Mongo */
set mapred.map.tasks.speculative.execution false
set mapred.reduce.tasks.speculative.execution false
define MongoStorage com.mongodb.hadoop.pig.MongoStorage(); /* Shortcut */

avros = load '$avros' using AvroStorage(); /* For example, 'enron.avro' */

store avros into '$mongourl' using MongoStorage(); /* For example,
'mongodb://localhost/enron.emails' */
```

If something goes wrong, you can always drop the store and try again. The beauty of our infrastructure is that everything is reproducible from the original data.

```
[bash]$ mongo agile_data

MongoDB shell version: 2.0.2
connecting to: agile_data

> db.emails.drop()
true
```

Finally, verify that our emails are in MongoDB:

```
> db.emails.findOne()

{
  "_id" : ObjectId("4fcd4748414efd682a861443"),
  "message_id" : "CANSvDjoPNg5E-hdBSDm5SCgn-AByKALr-Mi-szXRdmqu3g@mail.gmail.com",
  "thread_id" : "1403882181130881909",
  "in_reply_to" : null,
  "subject" : "Holla",
  "body" : "\r\n\r\n-- \r\nRussell Jurney twitter.com/rjurney
  russell.jurney@gmail.com datasyndrome.com\r\n",
  "date" : "2012-06-04T14:46:19",
  "froms" : [
    {
      "real_name" : "Russell Jurney",
      "address" : "russell.jurney@gmail.com"
    }
  ],
  "tos" : [
    {
      "real_name" : "Paul Stamatiou",
      "address" : "p@pstam.com"
    }
  ],
  "ccs" : null,
  "bccs" : null,
  "reply_tos" : null
}
```

Presenting Emails in a Browser

Now that we've published our emails to a document store, we're ready to present our data in a browser via a simple web application (Figure 5-4).

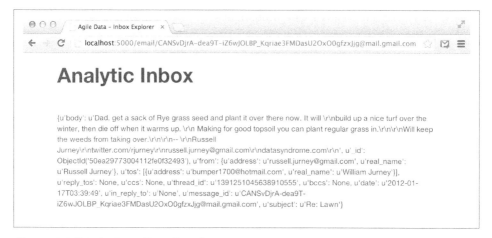

Figure 5-4. Displaying a Raw Email

Serving Emails with Flask and pymongo

Flask and pymongo make querying and returning emails easy. Jinja2 makes it easy to transform emails to web pages. Check out *ch05/web/index.py*.

```
from flask import Flask, render_template, request
import pymongo
import json, pyelasticsearch
import re
import config

# Set up Flask
app = Flask(__name__)

# Set up Mongo
conn = pymongo.Connection() # defaults to localhost
db = conn.agile_data
emails = db['emails']

# Set up ElasticSearch
elastic = pyelasticsearch.ElasticSearch(config.ELASTIC_URL)

# Controller: Fetch an email and display it
@app.route("/email/<message_id>")
def sent_counts(message_id):
  email = emails.find_one({'message_id': message_id})
  return render_template('partials/email.html', email=email)
```

Rendering HTML5 with Jinja2

Note that render_template in our example points at the file *ch05/web/templates/partials/email.html*. This is a partial template that fills in the dynamic content area of our layout page. The layout page that it subclasses, *ch05/web/templates/layout.html*, imports Bootstrap and handles the global design for each page, such as the header, overall styling, and footer. This saves us from repeating ourselves each page to create a consistent layout for the application.

The layout template contains an empty content block, {% block content %}{% end block %}, into which our partial template containing our application data is rendered.

```
<!-- Part 1: Wrap all page content here -->
    <div id="wrap">

        <!-- Begin page content -->
        <div class="container">
          {% block content %}{% endblock %}
        </div>

        <div id="push"></div>
    </div>

    <div id="footer">
```

Our email-specific partial template works by subclassing the layout template. The rest of the template is composed of macros. Jinja2 syntax and macros are simple enough.

Jinja2 templates perform control flow in {% %} tags to loop through tuples and arrays and apply conditionals. We display variables by putting bound data or arbitrary Python code inside the {{ }} tags. For example, our email template looks like this:

```
<!-- Extend our site layout -->
    {% extends "layout.html" %}

    <!-- Include our common macro set -->
    {% import "macros.jnj" as common %}

    <!-- Link to another message ID -->
    {% macro display_in_reply_to(key, name) %}
      {% if email[key] != 'None' -%}
        <div class="row">
          {{ common.display_label(name)|safe }}
          {{ common.display_link(email[key], '/email', email[key])|safe }}
        </div>
      {% endif -%}
    {% endmacro -%}

    <!-- Convert the carriage returns in the body to HTML endlines -->
    {% macro convert_body(body) -%}
      {{ body.replace('\r\n', '<br />')|safe }}
    {% endmacro -%}

    <!-- Display the email body -->
    {% macro display_email_body(record) -%}
      {% if(record['body']) -%}
```

```
        <div class="row">
          <div class="span" style="display: inline-block; margin-top: 17px;
           background-color: #F7F7F7; padding: 10px;">
            {{ convert_body(record['body']) }}
          </div>
        </div>
        {% endif -%}
      {% endmacro -%}

      <!-- Block in which content appears in superclass - layout.html -->
      {% block content -%}
        <div class="page-header">
          <h1>Analytic Inbox</h1>
        </div>
        <p class="lead">Email ID: {{email['message_id']}}</p>
        <div>
        {{ common.display_email_addresses('From', email['from'])|safe }}
        {{ common.display_email_addresses('To', email['tos'])|safe }}
        {{ common.display_email_addresses('Cc', email['ccs'])|safe }}
        {{ common.display_email_addresses('Bcc', email['bccs'])|safe }}
        {{ common.display_email_addresses('Reply-To',
           email['reply_tos'])|safe }}

        {{ display_in_reply_to('in_reply_to', 'In-Reply-To') }}
        {{ common.display_field(email['date'], 'Date')|safe }}
        {{ common.display_field(email['subject'], 'Subject')|safe }}

        {{ display_email_body(email) }}
        </div>
      {% endblock -%}
```

Our content block is our `main` code that calls on macros to render HTML for our data. To avoid repeating ourselves, each parametized HTML block is written by a macro. We start with a raw template, plug in values from our data (via the email variable we bound to the template), and get the page displaying some data. Then we remove repetition via macros until we duplicate as little logic as possible. This enables us to reuse macros later, and to make global changes that affect the entire page or application.

We can see the email in our web page with a `message_id`. To test things out, grab a `message_id` directly from MongoDB.

```
[bash]$ mongo agile_data

>db.emails.findOne()

{
"_id" : ObjectId("50ea29793004112fe0f33f4f"),
"message_id" : "4484555894252760987@unknownmsgid",
"thread_id" : "1386763841092409007",
"in_reply_to" : "None",
"subject" : "Re:",
"body" : "Dad, get a sack of Rye grass seed and
```

```
plant it over there now.  It\r\nwill build up a
nice turf over the winter, then die off when it
warms\r\nup.  Making for good topsoil you can
plant regular grass in.
\r\n\r\nWill keep the weeds from taking over.
\r\n\r\nRussell Jurney\r\ntwitter.com/rjurney\r\
nrussell.jurney@gmail.com\r\ndatasyndrome.com
\r\n\r\nOn Nov 28, 2011, at 2:19 PM, William Jurney
<*******@hotmail.com> wrote:\r\n\r\n> <mime-attachment>
\r\n> <photo.JPG>\r\n",
"date" : "2011-11-28T14:57:38",
"from" : {
"real_name" : "Russell Jurney",
"address" : "russell.jurney@gmail.com"
},
"tos" : [
{
"real_name" : "William Jurney",
"address" : "*******@hotmail.com"
}
],
"ccs" : null,
"bccs" : null,
"reply_tos" : null
}
```

We can now fetch a single email via *http://localhost:5000/email/[my_message_id]*, as shown in Figure 5-5.

Our Flask console shows the resources being accessed.

```
 * Running on http://127.0.0.1:5000/
 * Restarting with reloader
127.0.0.1 - - [12:40:08] "GET /email/%3my_message_id%3E HTTP/1.1" 200 -
127.0.0.1 - - [12:40:08] "GET /static/bootstrap/docs/assets/css/bootstrap.css
 HTTP/1.1" 304 -
127.0.0.1 - - [12:40:08] "GET /email/images/favicon.ico HTTP/1.1" 404 -
```

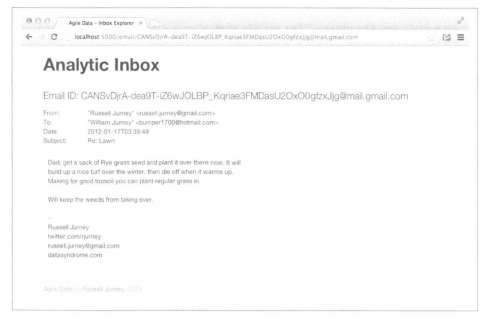

Figure 5-5. Presenting a single email

Great! But what have we achieved?

We've completed the base of the pyramid, level 1—displaying atomic records—in our standard data pipeline. This is a foundation. Whatever advanced analytics we offer, in the end, the user will often want to see the signal itself—that is, the raw data backing our inferences. There is no skipping steps here: if we can't correctly "visualize" a single atomic record, then our platform and strategy have no base. They are weak.

Agile Checkpoint

Since we now have working software, it is time to let users in to start getting their feedback. "Wait, really? This thing is embarrassing!" Get over yourself.

We all want to be Steve Jobs; we all want to have a devastating product launch, and to make a huge splash with a top-secret invention. But with analytics applications, when you hesitate to ship, you let your fragile ego undermine your ability to become Steve Jobs by worrying about not looking like him in your first draft. If you don't ship crap as step one, you're unlikely to get to a brilliant step 26.

You will notice immediately when you ship this (maybe to close friends or insiders who clone the source from GitHub at this point) that users can't find which email mes sage_ids to click on. To get real utility from this, we need list and search.

You may well have anticipated this. Why ship something obviously broken? Because although step two is obvious, *step 13 is not*. We must involve users at this step because their participation is a fundamental part of completing step one of the data-value pyramid. Users provide validation of our underlying assumptions, which at this stage might be stated as: does anyone care about email? Without validation, we haven't learned anything. Without learning, we are building in the dark. Success that way is unlikely, just as a pyramid without a strong foundation will soon crumble.

The other reason to ship something now is that the act of publishing, presenting, and sharing your work will highlight a number of problems in your platform setup that would otherwise go undiscovered until the moment you launch your product. In Agile Big Data, you *always ship* after a sprint. As a team member, you don't control whether to ship or not. You control what to ship and how broad an audience to release it to. This release might be appropriate for five friends and family members, and you might have to hound them to get it running. In doing so, you will optimize your packaging and resolve dependencies. You'll have to make it presentable. Without such work, without a clear deliverable to guide your efforts, technical issues you are blinded to by familiarity will be transparent to you.

Now, let's add listing emails and search so we can start generating real clicks from real users.

Listing Emails

An email inbox is typically presented as a time-sorted list, with the most recent emails first. A list helps bridge individual emails to other emails, and to link emails to a point in time represented by our place in the inbox. Lists are the next step after displaying individual records.

Listing Emails with MongoDB

Before we search our emails, we need the capacity to list them in order to display our search results. We can use MongoDB's query capabilities to return a list, sorted by time-stamp. Check out *ch05/list_emails.mongo.js*.

```
mongo agile_data
  > db.emails.find().sort({date:1})
  error: {
    "$err" : "too much data for sort() with no index.  add an index or specify a
              smaller limit",
    "code" : 10128
  }
```

Whoops! No index. We must create one to sort by date.

```
  > db.emails.getIndexes()
  [
```

```
    {
      "v" : 1,
      "key" : {
        "_id" : 1
      },
      "ns" : "agile_data.emails",
      "name" : "_id_"
    }
]

> db.emails.ensureIndex({date: 1})
> db.emails.getIndexes()
[
    {
      "v" : 1,
      "key" : {
        "_id" : 1
      },
      "ns" : "agile_data.emails",
      "name" : "_id_"
    },
    {
      "v" : 1,
      "key" : {
        "date" : 1
      },
      "ns" : "agile_data.emails",
      "name" : "date_1"
    }
]
```

While we're at it, let's add an index for message_id.

```
> db.emails.ensureIndex({message_id: 1})
```

Now that our index on dates is in place, we can get the last 10 emails sent to us in pretty
JSON format.

```
> db.emails.find().sort({date:0}).limit(10).pretty()
{
        {
        "_id" : ObjectId("4f7a5da2414e4dd0645d1176"),
        "message_id":"<CA+bvURyn-rLcH_JRNq+YJ_Hkvhnrpk8zfYshL-wA@mail.gmail.com>",
        "from" : [

    ...
```

Our Flask stub has two default routes that display the most recent 20 emails, unless
specified by arguments. Otherwise, it works the same as before—except this time it
passes an array of emails instead of one email. Check out *ch05/web/index.py* (Figure 5-6).

```
@app.route('/')
@app.route('/emails/')
```

```
@app.route("/emails/<int:offset1>/<int:offset2>")
def list_emails(offset1 = 0, offset2 = 20):
  offset1 = int(offset1)
  offset2 = int(offset2)
  emails = emaildb.find()[offset1:offset2] # Uses a MongoDB cursor
  return render_template('partials/emails.html', emails=emails)
```

Our templates are pretty simple too, owing to Bootstrap's snazzy presentation of tables. Tables are often scoffed at, but this is tabular data, so their use is appropriate.

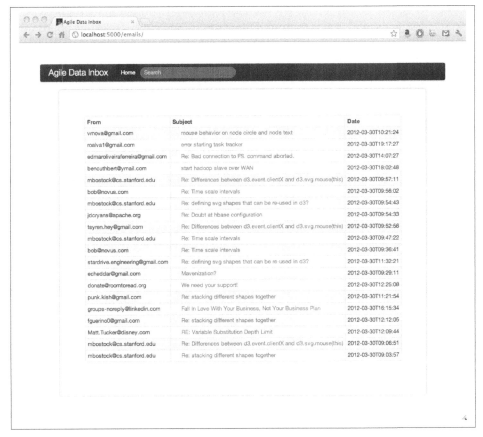

Figure 5-6. Presenting a list of emails

Anatomy of a Presentation

Now that we can list the most recent emails, our users say, "What if I want to see more than the last 20?" Shouldn't there be a previous/next button to scroll forward and back in time? Yes. That is what we add next.

So far we've glossed over how we're creating these templates, subtemplates, and macros. Now we're going to dive in by creating a macro and a subtemplate for pagination.

Reinventing the wheel?

Why are we building our own pagination? Isn't that a solved problem?

The first answer is that it makes a good example to connect the browser with the data directly. In Agile Big Data, we try to process the data into the very state it takes on a user's screen with minimal manipulation between the backend and an image in a browser. Why? We do this because it decreases complexity in our systems, because it unites data scientist and designer around the same vision, and because this philosophy embraces the nature of distributed systems in that it doesn't rely on joins or other tricks that work best on "big iron"—or legacy systems.

Keeping the model consistent with the view is critical when the model is complex, as in a predictive system. We can best create value when the interaction design around a feature is cognizant of and consistent with the underlying data model. Data scientists must bring understanding of the data to the rest of the team, or the team can't build to a common vision. The principle of building view to the model ensures this from the beginning.

In practice, we cannot predict at which layer a feature will arise. It may first appear as a burst of creativity from a web developer, designer, data scientist, or platform engineer. To validate it, we must ship it in an experiment as quickly as possible, and so the implementation layer of a feature may in fact begin at any level of our stack. When this happens, we must take note and ticket the feature as containing technical debt. As the feature stabilizes, if it is to remain in the system, we move it further back in the stack as time permits.

A full-blown application framework like Rails or Django would likely build in this functionality. However, when we are building an application around derived data, the mechanics of interactions often vary in both subtle and dramatic ways. Frameworks offer less value in these situations, where their behavior must likely be customized. Also note that while MongoDB happens to include the ability to select and return a range of sorted records, the NoSQL store you use may or may not provide this functionality, or it may not be possible to use this feature because publishing your data in a timely manner requires a custom service. You may have to precompute the data periodically and serve the list yourself. NoSQL gives us options, and web frameworks are optimized for relational databases. We must often take matters into our own hands.

Prototyping back from HTML

Being familiar with email, we know scrolling forward and back is a solved problem (Figure 5-7).

Figure 5-7. Missing next/previous links

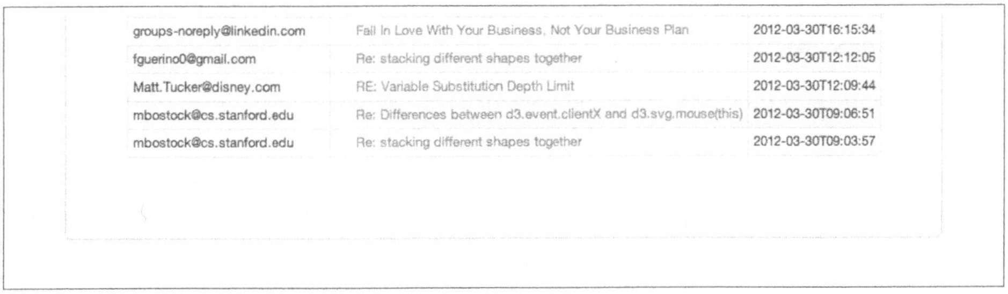

We need a previous/next button at the bottom of the page that links us to the previous/next *N* emails, if that range exists. Recall that we defined the email list API as follows (see *ch05/web/index.py*):

```
@app.route('/')
@app.route('/emails/')
@app.route("/emails/<int:offset1>/<int:offset2>")
def list_emails(offset1 = 0, offset2 = config.EMAILS_PER_PAGE):
  email_list = emails.find()[offset1:offset2]
  nav_offsets = get_navigation_offsets(offset1, offset2, config.EMAILS_PER_PAGE)
  return render_template('partials/emails.html', emails=email_list, nav_offsets=
  nav_offsets, nav_path='/emails/', query=query)
```

This means that all we need is a link to an incremented/decremented offset range for the path */emails/offset1/offset2*. Let's prototype the feature based on these requirements by appending static forward and back links against our email list API.

For example, we want to dynamically render this HTML, corresponding to the URL */emails/20/40*, as shown in Figure 5-8:

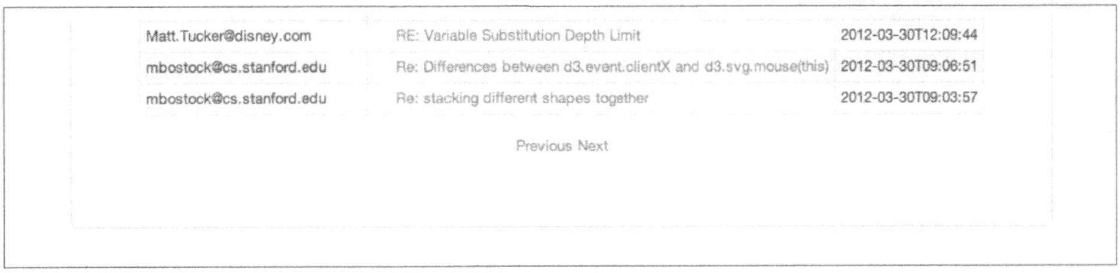

Figure 5-8. Simple next/previous links

templates/partials/emails.html

```
...
  </table>
  <div style="text-align: center">
    <a href="/emails/0/20">Previous</a>
    <a href="/emails/40/60">Next</a>
```

```
  </div>
{% endblock -%}
```

Pasting and navigating to the links, such as *http://localhost:5000/emails/40/60*, demonstrates that the feature works with our data.

Now let's generalize it. Macros are convenient, but we don't want to make our template too complicated, so we compute the increments in a Python helper (we might consider a model class) and make a macro to render the offsets.

For starters, let's use this opportunity to set up a simple config file to set variables like the number of emails to display per page. Embedding these in code will cause headaches later.

config.py
```
# config.py, a configuration file for index.py
EMAIL_PER_PAGE = 20
```

Let's also create a simple helper to calculate email offsets. In time this will become a full-blown class model, but for now, we'll just create a helpers section in *index.py*.

The controller now binds the navigation variables to the template, because we are now passing both the list of emails and the calculated offsets for the navigation links.

index.py
```
# Simple configuration
import config

# Calculate email offsets for fetchig lists of emails from MongoDB
def get_navigation_offsets(offset1, offset2, increment):
  offsets = {}
  offsets['Next'] = {'top_offset': offset2 + increment, 'bottom_offset':
  offset1 + increment}
  offsets['Previous'] = {'top_offset': max(offset2 - increment, 0),
  'bottom_offset': max(offset1 - increment, 0)} # Don't go < 0
  return offsets

...

# Enable /emails and /emails/ to serve the last 20 emails in our inbox unless
otherwise specified
default_offsets={'offset1': 0, 'offset2': 20}
@app.route('/emails', defaults=default_offsets)
@app.route('/emails/', defaults=default_offsets)
@app.route("/emails/<int:offset1>/<int:offset2>")
def list_emaildb(offset1=0, offset2=config.EMAILS_PER_PAGE):
  emails = emaildb.find()[offset1:offset2] # Uses a MongoDB cursor
  nav_offsets = get_offsets(offset1, offset2, config.EMAIL_RANGE)
  return render_template('partials/emails.html', emails=emails, nav_offsets=
  nav_offsets, nav_path='/emails/')
```

Our email list template calls a macro to render our data. Note the use of |safe to ensure our HTML isn't escaped:

templates/partials/emails.html

```
...
  <div>
    <table class="table table-striped table-condensed">
      <thead>
        <th>From</th>
        <th>Subject</th>
        <th>Date</th>
      </thead>
      <tbody>
        {% for email in emails %}
        <tr style="white-space:nowrap;">
          <td>{{ common.display_email_address(email['from'])|safe }}</td>
          <td>{{ common.display_link(email['message_id'], '/email', email
                ['subject'])|safe }}</td>
          <td style="white-space:nowrap;">{{ email['date'] }}</td>
        </tr>
        {% endfor %}
      </tbody>
    </table>
    {% if nav_offsets and nav_path -%}
      {{ common.display_nav(nav_offsets, nav_path, query)|safe }}
    {% endif -%}
  </div>
```

which we place in our Jinja2 macros file, further breaking up the task as the drawing of two links inside a div.

templates/macros.jnj

```
<!-- Display two navigation links for previous/next page in the email list -->
{% macro display_nav(offsets, path, query) -%}
  <div style="text-align: center;">
    {% for key, values in offsets.items() -%}
      {% if values['bottom_offset'] >= 0 -%}
        <a style="margin-left: 20px; margin-right: 20px;" href="{{ path }}{{ values
        ['bottom_offset'] }}/{{ values['top_offset'] }}{%- if query -%}?search=
        {{query}}{%- endif -%}">{{ key }}</a>
      {% else -%}
        {{ key }}
      {% endif -%}
    {% endfor -%}
  </div>
{% endmacro -%}
```

And we're done. We can now paginate through our list of emails as we would in any other inbox. We're one step closer to providing the kind of user experience that will enable real user sessions, and we've extended a graph connecting emails over the top of our individual records. This additional structure will enable even more structure later on, as we climb the stack.

Searching Our Email

Browsing through a list of emails certainly beats manually looking up `message_ids`, but it's hardly as efficient as search for finding emails of interest to a particular topic. Let's use our data platform to add search.

Indexing Our Email with Pig, ElasticSearch, and Wonderdog

Remember from Chapter 3 that we can index our emails for search easily with Pig and Wonderdog, as shown in Example 5-3.

 Check out Infochimps, which developed Wonderdog as part of its big data platform: *http://www.infochimps.com/platform*.

Example 5-3. Process and searchify email data

```
/* Avro uses json-simple, and is in piggybank until Pig 0.12, where AvroStorage and
TrevniStorage are builtins */
REGISTER $HOME/pig/build/ivy/lib/Pig/avro-1.5.3.jar
REGISTER $HOME/pig/build/ivy/lib/Pig/json-simple-1.1.jar
REGISTER $HOME/pig/contrib/piggybank/java/piggybank.jar

DEFINE AvroStorage org.apache.pig.piggybank.storage.avro.AvroStorage();

/* Elasticsearch's own jars */
REGISTER $HOME/elasticsearch-0.20.2/lib/*.jar

/* Register wonderdog - elasticsearch integration */
REGISTER $HOME/wonderdog/target/wonderdog-1.0-SNAPSHOT.jar

/* Remove the old email json */
rmf /tmp/inbox_json

/* Nuke the elasticsearch emails index, as we are about to replace it. */
sh curl -XDELETE 'http://localhost:9200/inbox/emails'

/* Load Avros, and store as JSON */
emails = LOAD '/me/Data/test_mbox' USING AvroStorage();
STORE emails INTO '/tmp/inbox_json' USING JsonStorage();

/* Now load the JSON as a single chararray field, and index it into ElasticSearch
with Wonderdog from InfoChimps */
email_json = LOAD '/tmp/inbox_json' AS (email:chararray);
STORE email_json INTO 'es://inbox/emails?json=true&size=1000' USING com.infochimps
.elasticsearch.pig.ElasticSearchStorage(
  '$HOME/elasticsearch-0.20.2/config/elasticsearch.yml',
  '$HOME/elasticsearch-0.20.2/plugins');
```

```
/* Search for Hadoop to make sure we get a hit in our email index */
sh curl -XGET 'http://localhost:9200/inbox/emails/_search?q=hadoop&
pretty=true&size=1'
```

Test things out with a search query:

```
[bash]$ curl -XGET 'http://localhost:9200/email/email/_search?q=hadoop&pretty=
true&size=1'
```

If you want to reload your data after changing it, you can get rid of an index easily:

```
[bash]$ curl -XDELETE 'http://localhost:9200/email/'
```

Searching Our Email on the Web

Next, let's connect our search engine to the Web.

First, configure pyelastic to point at our ElasticSearch server.

```
config.py
ELASTIC_URL = 'http://localhost:9200/inbox'
```

Then import, set up, and query ElasticSearch via the /emails/search path.

```
index.py
# ElasticSearch
import json, pyelasticsearch

...

# Set up ElasticSearch onnection
elastic = pyelasticsearch.ElasticSearch(config.ELASTIC_URL)

...

# Process elasticsearch hits and return email records
def process_search(results):
  emails = []
  if results['hits'] and results['hits']['hits']:
    hits = results['hits']['hits']
    for hit in hits:
      email = hit['_source']
      emails.append(email)
  return emails

# Controller: Fetch a list of emails and display them
@app.route('/')
@app.route('/emails/')
@app.route("/emails/<int:offset1>/<int:offset2>")
def list_emails(offset1 = 0, offset2 = config.EMAILS_PER_PAGE, query=None):
  query = request.args.get('search')
  if query==None:
    email_list = emails.find()[offset1:offset2]
```

```
else:
  results = elastic.search({'query': {'match': { '_all': query}},
  'sort': {'date': {'order': 'desc'}}, 'from': offset1, 'size':
    config.EMAILS_PER_PAGE}, index="emails")
  print results
  email_list = process_search(results)
nav_offsets = get_navigation_offsets(offset1, offset2, config.EMAILS_PER_PAGE)
return render_template('partials/emails.html', emails=email_list,
  nav_offsets=nav_offsets, nav_path='/emails/', query=query)
```

Generalizing the navigation links, we are able to use the same template for both listing emails in order and searching them. Our search box is part of our layout template (*ch05/ web/templates/layout.html*), and we need only set its action to point at our search API (see Figure 5-9).

layout.html
```
<form class="navbar-search pull-right">
  <input name="search" type="text" class="search-query" placeholder="Search"
  value="{% if query -%}{{query}} {% endif -%}">
</form>
```

Figure 5-9. Searching for emails

Conclusion

We have now collected, published, indexed, displayed, listed, and searched our emails. They are no longer abstract. We can search for keywords, click on individual emails, and explore our inbox as we might in an email client. More important, we have piped our raw data through our platform and transformed it into an interactive application.

This application forms the base of our value stack. We will use it as the way to develop, present, and iterate on more advanced features throughout the book as we build value walking up the data-value pyramid. With this base of the data-value pyramid in place, we move on to building charts.

## CHAPTER 6

Visualizing Data with Charts

In the next step, our second agile sprint, we will start building charts from our data (Figure 6-1).

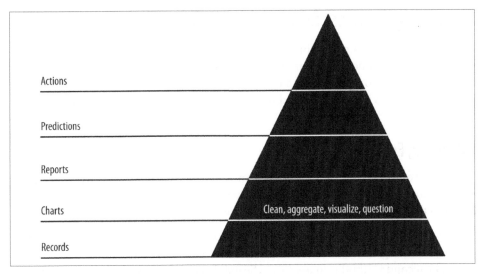

Figure 6-1. Level 2: visualizing with charts

Charts are our first view into our data in aggregate, mapping the properties of many records into visual representations that help us understand and navigate further and expose entities and concepts in our data. Our goals in this step are to publish charts to generate interest in our data and get users interacting with it, to build reusable tools that will help us explore our data interactively in reports in the next step, and to begin extracting structure and entities from our data so that we can create new features and insights with this structure.

Code examples for this chapter are available at *https://github.com/rjurney/Agile_Data_Code/tree/master/ch06*. Clone the repository and follow along!

```
git clone https://github.com/rjurney/Agile_Data_Code.git
```

Good Charts

A good chart is anything users find interesting enough to visualize and that users respond to. Expect to throw many charts away until you find good ones—don't try to specify them up front or you will be disappointed. Instead, try to use your intuition and curiosity to add charts organically.

You can create charts in an ad hoc way at first, but as you progress, your workflow should become increasingly automated and reproducible.

Well-formed URLs with slugs generalize, so one chart works for anything. Good charts are those that get clicked, so get users involved. Later, we'll improve and extend successful charts into interactive reports.

Extracting Entities: Email Addresses

An email address is an ego acting through a certain address or context (this is a simplification, because one person may have multiple email addresses, but an email address is a reasonable approximation of an ego). In this chapter, we will create a new entity for each email address in our inbox and then create interesting data to chart, display, and interact with.

Extracting Emails

We start by creating an index of all emails in which any given email address appears in the *from/to/cc/bcc* fields. This is a pattern: when you're creating a new entity, always first link it to the atomic base records. Note that we can achieve this mapping in two ways.

The first option is using Pig to group emails by email addresses. This method puts all of our processing at the far backend in batch, which could be desirable for very large data. The second method is to use ElasticSearch Facets to query our email index just as we have before, but with different handling in our web application.

We group our emails in Pig and store them in MongoDB. We do this because we intend to use this data in other features via JOINs, and while Wonderdog enables reading data from ElasticSearch, it is important to have a copy of this data on reliable bulk storage, where it is truly persistent. We know we can easily and arbitrarily scale operations on Hadoop.

We'll need to project each *to/from/cc/bcc* address with the message ID of that email, merge these header/address parts together by email, and then group by address to get a list of message IDs per address, and a list of addresses per message ID. Check out *ch06/ emails_per_address.pig*, as shown in Example 6-1.

Example 6-1. Messages per email address

```
/* Avro uses json-simple, and is in piggybank until Pig 0.12, where AvroStorage and
TrevniStorage are builtins */
REGISTER $HOME/pig/build/ivy/lib/Pig/avro-1.5.3.jar
REGISTER $HOME/pig/build/ivy/lib/Pig/json-simple-1.1.jar
REGISTER $HOME/pig/contrib/piggybank/java/piggybank.jar

DEFINE AvroStorage org.apache.pig.piggybank.storage.avro.AvroStorage();

/* MongoDB libraries and configuration */
REGISTER $HOME/mongo-hadoop/mongo-2.10.1.jar
REGISTER $HOME/mongo-hadoop/core/target/mongo-hadoop-core-1.1.0-SNAPSHOT.jar
REGISTER $HOME/mongo-hadoop/pig/target/mongo-hadoop-pig-1.1.0-SNAPSHOT.jar

DEFINE MongoStorage com.mongodb.hadoop.pig.MongoStorage();

set default_parallel 10
set mapred.map.tasks.speculative.execution false
set mapred.reduce.tasks.speculative.execution false

/* Macro to filter emails according to existence of header pairs:
[from, to, cc, bcc, reply_to]
Then project the header part, message_id, and subject, and emit them, lowercased.

Note: you can't paste macros into Grunt as of Pig 0.11. You will have to execute
this file. */
DEFINE headers_messages(email, col) RETURNS set {
  filtered = FILTER $email BY ($col IS NOT NULL);
  flat = FOREACH filtered GENERATE
  FLATTEN($col.address) AS $col, message_id, subject, date;
  lowered = FOREACH flat GENERATE LOWER($col) AS address, message_id,
  subject, date;
  $set = FILTER lowered BY (address IS NOT NULL) and (address != '') and
  (date IS NOT NULL);
}

/* Nuke the Mongo stores, as we are about to replace it. */
-- sh mongo agile_data --quiet --eval 'db.emails_per_address.drop(); exit();'
-- sh mongo agile_data --quiet --eval 'db.addresses_per_email.drop(); exit();'

rmf /tmp/emails_per_address.json

emails = load '/me/Data/test_mbox' using AvroStorage();
froms = foreach emails generate LOWER(from.address) as address, message_id, subject,
date;
froms = filter froms by (address IS NOT NULL) and (address != '') and
(date IS NOT NULL);
tos = headers_messages(emails, 'tos');
```

```
ccs = headers_messages(emails, 'ccs');
bccs = headers_messages(emails, 'bccs');
reply_tos = headers_messages(emails, 'reply_tos');

address_messages = UNION froms, tos, ccs, bccs, reply_tos;

/* Messages per email address, sorted by date desc. Limit to 50 to ensure rapid
access. */
emails_per_address = foreach (group address_messages by address) {
                                address_messages = order address_messages by date desc;
                                top_50 = limit address_messages 50;
                                generate group as address,
                                        top_50.(message_id, subject, date) as emails;
                                }

store emails_per_address into 'mongodb://localhost/agile_data.emails_per_address'
using MongoStorage();

/* Email addresses per email */
addresses_per_email = foreach (group address_messages by message_id) generate group
as message_id, address_messages.(address) as addresses;
store addresses_per_email into 'mongodb://localhost/agile_data.addresses_per_email'
using MongoStorage();
```

Now we'll check on our data in MongoDB. Check out *ch06/mongo.js*.

```
$ mongo agile_data
MongoDB shell version: 2.0.2
connecting to: agile_data
> show collections
addresses_per_id
ids_per_address
...

> db.emails_per_address.findOne()
{
  "_id" : ObjectId("4ff7a38a0364f2e2dd6a43bc"),
  "group" : "bob@clownshoes.org",
  "email_address_messages" : [
    {
      "email_address" : "bob@clownshoes.org",
      "message_id" : "B526D4C4-AA05-4A61-A0C5-9CF77373995C@123.org"
    },
    {
      "email_address" : "bob@clownshoes.org",
      "message_id" : "E58C12BA-0985-448B-BCD7-6C6C364FCF15@123.org"
    },
    {
      "email_address" : "bob@clownshoes.org",
      "message_id" : "593B0552-D007-453D-A3A8-B10288638E50@123.org"
    },
    {
      "email_address" : "bob@clownshoes.org",
```

```
    "message_id" : "3A211C33-FE82-4B2C-BE2F-16D5F7EB3A9C@123.org"
    }
  ]
}

> db.addresses_per_email.findOne()
{
"_id" : ObjectId("50f71a5530047b9226f0dcb3"),
"message_id" : "4484555894252760987@unknownmsgid",
"addresses" : [
{
"address" : "russell.jurney@gmail.com"
},
{
"address" : "*******@hotmail.com"
}
]
}

> db.addresses_per_email.find({'email_address_messages': {$size: 4}})[0]
{
  "_id" : ObjectId("4ff7ad800364f868d343e557"),
  "message_id" : "4F586853.40903@touk.pl",
  "email_address_messages" : [
    {
      "email_address" : "user@pig.apache.org",
      "message_id" : "4F586853.40903@touk.pl"
    },
    {
      "email_address" : "bob@plantsitting.org",
      "message_id" : "4F586853.40903@touk.pl"
    },
    {
      "email_address" : "billgraham@gmail.com",
      "message_id" : "4F586853.40903@touk.pl"
    },
    {
      "email_address" : "dvryaboy@gmail.com",
      "message_id" : "4F586853.40903@touk.pl"
    }
  ]
}
```

We can see how to query email addresses per message and messages per email address.
This kind of data is foundational—it lets us add features to a page by directly rendering precomputed data. We'll start by displaying these email addresses as a word cloud as part of the */email* controller:

```
# Controller: Fetch an email and display it
@app.route("/email/<message_id>")
def email(message_id):
  email = emails.find_one({'message_id': message_id})
```

```
addresses = addresses_per_email.find_one({'message_id': message_id})
return render_template('partials/email.html', email=email,
  addresses=addresses['addresses'],
  chart_json=json.dumps(sent_dist_records['sent_distribution']))
```

Our template is simple. It extends our application layout and relies on Bootstrap for styling.

```
{% if addresses -%}
  <h3 style="margin-bottom: 5px;">Email Addresses</h2>
  <ul class="nav nav-pills">
    {% for item in addresses -%}
    <li class="active">
      <a style="margin: 3px;" href="/address/{{ item['address'] }}
          ">{{ item['address'] }}</a>
    </li>
    {% endfor -%}
  </ul>
{% endif -%}
```

And the result is simple:

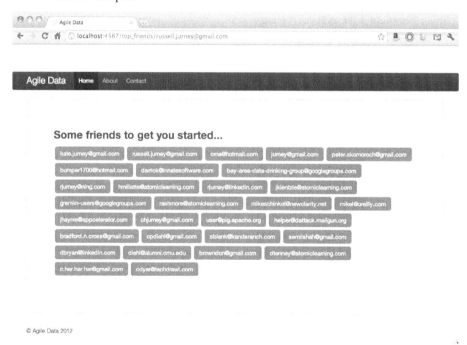

Visualizing Time

Let's continue by computing a distribution of the times each email address sends emails. Check out *ch06/sent_distributions.pig*.

```
/* Set Home Directory - where we install software */
%default HOME `echo \$HOME/Software/`

/* Avro uses json-simple, and is in piggybank until Pig 0.12, where AvroStorage
and TrevniStorage are builtins */
REGISTER $HOME/pig/build/ivy/lib/Pig/avro-1.5.3.jar
REGISTER $HOME/pig/build/ivy/lib/Pig/json-simple-1.1.jar
REGISTER $HOME/pig/contrib/piggybank/java/piggybank.jar

DEFINE AvroStorage org.apache.pig.piggybank.storage.avro.AvroStorage();
DEFINE substr org.apache.pig.piggybank.evaluation.string.SUBSTRING();
DEFINE tohour org.apache.pig.piggybank.evaluation.datetime.truncate.ISOToHour();

/* MongoDB libraries and configuration */
REGISTER $HOME/mongo-hadoop/mongo-2.10.1.jar
REGISTER $HOME/mongo-hadoop/core/target/mongo-hadoop-core-1.1.0-SNAPSHOT.jar
REGISTER $HOME/mongo-hadoop/pig/target/mongo-hadoop-pig-1.1.0-SNAPSHOT.jar

DEFINE MongoStorage com.mongodb.hadoop.pig.MongoStorage();

set default_parallel 5
set mapred.map.tasks.speculative.execution false
set mapred.reduce.tasks.speculative.execution false

/* Macro to extract the hour portion of an iso8601 datetime string */
define extract_time(relation, field_in, field_out) RETURNS times {
  $times = foreach $relation generate flatten($field_in.(address)) as $field_out,
                          substr(tohour(date), 11, 13) as sent_hour;
};

rmf /tmp/sent_distributions.avro

emails = load '/me/Data/test_mbox' using AvroStorage();
filtered = filter emails BY (from is not null) and (date is not null);

/* Some emails that users send to have no from entries, list email lists.  These
addresses have reply_to's associated with them.  Here we split reply_to
processing off to ensure reply_to addresses get credit for sending emails. */
split filtered into has_reply_to if (reply_tos is not null), froms if (reply_tos
is null);

/* For emails with a reply_to, count both the from and the reply_to as a sender. */
reply_to = extract_time(has_reply_to, reply_tos, from);
reply_to_froms = extract_time(has_reply_to, from, from);
froms = extract_time(froms, from, from);
all_froms = union reply_to, reply_to_froms, froms;

pairs = foreach all_froms generate LOWER(from) as sender_email_address,
                               sent_hour;

sent_times = foreach (group pairs by (sender_email_address, sent_hour)) generate
  flatten(group) as (sender_email_address, sent_hour),
```

```
                                                    COUNT_STAR(pairs) as total;

/* Note the use of a sort inside a foreach block */
sent_distributions = foreach (group sent_times by sender_email_address) {
    solid = filter sent_times by (sent_hour is not null) and (total is not null);
    sorted = order solid by sent_hour;
    generate group as address, sorted.(sent_hour, total) as sent_distribution;
};

store sent_distributions into '/tmp/sent_distributions.avro' using AvroStorage();
store sent_distributions into 'mongodb://localhost/agile_data.sent_distributions'
using MongoStorage();
```

 Datetimes in Pig are in ISO8601 format for a reason: that format is text sortable and manipulatable via truncation. In this case, we are truncating to the hour and then reading the hour figure.

```
substr(tohour(date), 11, 13) as sent_hour
```

Now, plumb the data to a browser with Flask:

```
# Display sent distributions for a give email address
@app.route('/sent_distribution/<string:sender>')
def sent_distribution(sender):
  sent_dist_records = sent_distributions.find_one({'address': sender})
  return render_template('partials/sent_distribution.html',
  sent_distribution=sent_dist_records)
```

We start with a simple table in our Jinja2 HTML template, helped along by Bootstrap. Check out *ch06/web/templates/partials/email.html*.

```
{% if sent_distribution -%}
    <div class="span2">
      <table class="table table-striped table-condensed">
        <thead>
          <th>Hour</th>
          <th>Total Sent</th>
        </thead>
        <tbody>
          {% for item in sent_distribution['sent_distribution'] %}
          <tr style="white-space:nowrap;">
            <td>{{ item['sent_hour'] }}</td>
            <td style="white-space:nowrap;">{{ item['total'] }}</td>
          </tr>
          {% endfor %}
        </tbody>
      </table>
    </div>
  </div>
  <div class="row">
```

```
</div>
{% endif -%}
```

We can already tell our author is a night owl, but the shape of the distribution isn't very clear in Figure 6-2.

Hour	Total Sent
00	0
01	0
02	0
03	0
04	0
05	1
06	0
07	4
08	6
09	3
10	10
11	7
12	8
13	11
14	10
15	9
16	10
17	12
18	7
19	1
20	9
21	5
22	5
23	1

Figure 6-2. Emails sent by hour table

To get a better view of the visualization, we create a simple bar chart using d3.js and nvd3.js, based on this example: *http://mbostock.github.com/d3/tutorial/bar-1.html*.

Now we update our web app to produce JSON for d3.

```
# Display sent distributions for a give email address
@app.route('/sent_distribution/<string:sender>')
```

```python
def sent_distribution(sender):
    sent_dist_records = sent_distributions.find_one({'address': sender})
    return render_template('partials/sent_distribution.html',
        chart_json=json.dumps(sent_dist_records['sent_distribution']),
        sent_distribution=sent_dist_records)
```

And create the chart using nvd3:

```
{% if sent_distribution -%}
    <h3 style="margin-bottom: 5px;">Emails Sent by Hour</h2>
    <h5>{{ sent_distribution['address'] }}</h5>
    <div id="chart">
      <svg></svg>
    </div>
    <script>
    // Custom color function to highlight mode of the data
    var data = [{"key": "Test Chart", "values": {{ chart_json|safe }}}];
    var defaultColor = '#08C';
    var myColor = function(d, i) {
       return defaultColor;
     }
    nv.addGraph(function() {
    var chart = nv.models.discreteBarChart()
       .x(function(d) { return d.sent_hour })
       .y(function(d) { return d.total })
       .staggerLabels(true)
       .tooltips(false)
       .showValues(false)
       .color(myColor)
       .width(350)
       .height(300)

    d3.select('#chart svg')
       .datum(data)
     .transition().duration(500)
       .call(chart);

    nv.utils.windowResize(chart.update);

    return chart;
    });
    </script>
{% endif -%}
```

The resulting chart isn't perfect, but it is good enough to see a trend, which is precisely what we're after: enabling pattern recognition (Figure 6-3). To do so, we build the minimal amount of "shiny" needed so that our "ugly" is not distracting from the data underlying the charts. And while we could build this without putting it on the Web, doing so is what drives Agile Big Data: we get users, friends, and coworkers involved early, and we get the team communicating in the same realm immediately. We can build and release continuously and let designers design around data, engineers build around data, and data scientists publish data—right into the working application.

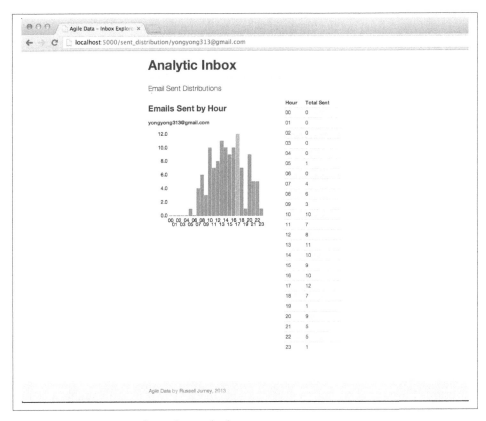

Figure 6-3. Histogram of emails sent by hour

This chart interests me because it shows different distributions even for people in the same time zone—morning people and night people.

 When you're choosing colors for charts, *http://www.colorpicker.com/* can be very helpful.

Our goal in creating charts is to draw early adopters to our application, so a good chart is something that interests real users. Along this line, we must ask ourselves: why would someone care about this data? How can we make it personally relevant? Step one is simply displaying the data in recognizable form. Step two is to highlight an interesting feature.

Accordingly, we add a new feature. We color the mode (the most common hour to send emails) in a lighter blue to highlight its significance: email this user at this time, and he is most likely to be around to see it.

We can dynamically affect the histogram's bars with a conditional `fill` function. When a bar's value matches the maximum, shade it light blue; otherwise, set the default color (Figure 6-4).

```
var defaultColor = '#08C';
var modeColor = '#4CA9F5';
var maxy = d3.max(data[0]['values'], function(d) { return d.total; });
var myColor = function(d, i) {
   if(d['total'] == maxy) { return modeColor; }
   else { return defaultColor; }
 }
```

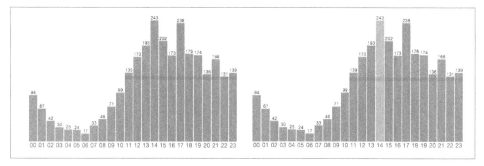

Figure 6-4. Histogram with mode highlighted

Illustrating the most likely hour a user sends email tells you when you might catch her online, and that is interesting. But to really grab the user's attention with this chart, we need to make it personally relevant. Why should I care what time a person I know emails unless I know whether she is in sync with me?

Conclusion

In this chapter, we've started to tease structure from our data with charts. In doing so, we have gone further than the preceding chapter in cataloging our data assets. We'll take what we've learned with us as we proceed up the data-value pyramid.

Now we move on to the next step of the data-value stack: *reports*.

## CHAPTER 7

Exploring Data with Reports

In the next step, our third agile sprint, we'll extend our chart pages into full-blown reports (Figure 7-1). In this step, charts become interactive, static pages become dynamic, and our data becomes explorable through networks of linked, related entities with charts. These are the characteristics of the reports stage of the data-value pyramid.

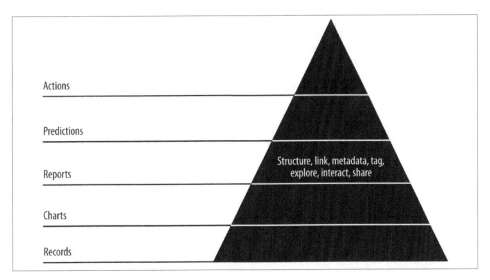

Figure 7-1. Level 3: exploring with reports

Code examples for this chapter are available at *https://github.com/rjurney/ Agile_Data_Code/tree/master/ch07*. Clone the repository and follow along!

```
git clone https://github.com/rjurney/Agile_Data_Code.git
```

Building Reports with Multiple Charts

To build a report, we need to compose multiple views on the same entity. The charts we made in the previous chapter will serve us well as we increase interactivity to create reports. Let's create an email address entity page and add a tag cloud for related emails to give us something closer to a report.

We'll start by creating a relation that shows the most related email addresses. Check out *ch07/pig/related_email_addresses.pig.*

```
/* Set Home Directory - where we install software */
%default HOME `echo \$HOME/Software/`

/* Avro uses json-simple, and is in piggybank until Pig 0.12, where AvroStorage
and TrevniStorage are Pig builtins */
REGISTER $HOME/pig/build/ivy/lib/Pig/avro-1.5.3.jar
REGISTER $HOME/pig/build/ivy/lib/Pig/json-simple-1.1.jar
REGISTER $HOME/pig/contrib/piggybank/java/piggybank.jar

DEFINE AvroStorage org.apache.pig.piggybank.storage.avro.AvroStorage();
DEFINE substr org.apache.pig.piggybank.evaluation.string.SUBSTRING();
DEFINE tohour org.apache.pig.piggybank.evaluation.datetime.truncate.ISOToHour();

/* MongoDB libraries and configuration */
REGISTER $HOME/mongo-hadoop/mongo-2.10.1.jar
REGISTER $HOME/mongo-hadoop/core/target/mongo-hadoop-core-1.1.0-SNAPSHOT.jar
REGISTER $HOME/mongo-hadoop/pig/target/mongo-hadoop-pig-1.1.0-SNAPSHOT.jar

DEFINE MongoStorage com.mongodb.hadoop.pig.MongoStorage();

set default_parallel 5
set mapred.map.tasks.speculative.execution false
set mapred.reduce.tasks.speculative.execution false

rmf /tmp/related_addresses.txt

emails = load '/me/Data/test_mbox' using AvroStorage();
/* We need to insert reply_to as a valid from or email addresses will miss in
our index */
split emails into has_reply_to if (reply_tos is not null), just_froms if
(reply_tos is null);
/* Count both the from and reply_to as valid froms if there is a reply_tos
field */
reply_tos = foreach has_reply_to generate FLATTEN(reply_tos.address) as from,
tos, ccs, bccs;
reply_to_froms = foreach has_reply_to generate from.address as from, tos,
ccs, bccs;
/* Treat emails without reply_to as normal */
just_froms = foreach just_froms generate from.address as from, tos, ccs, bccs;
/* Now union them all and we have our dataset to compute on */
all_froms = union reply_tos, reply_to_froms, just_froms;
```

```
/* Now pair up our froms/reply_tos with all recipient types,
   and union them to get a sender/recipient connection list. */
tos = foreach all_froms generate flatten(from) as from,
flatten(tos.address) as to;
ccs = foreach all_froms generate flatten(from) as from,
flatten(ccs.address) as to;
bccs = foreach all_froms generate flatten(from) as from,
flatten(bccs.address) as to;
pairs = union tos, ccs, bccs;

counts = foreach (group pairs by (from, to)) generate flatten(group) as (
from, to),
                                         COUNT(pairs) as total;

top_pairs = foreach (group counts by from) {
  filtered = filter counts by (to is not null);
  sorted = order filtered by total desc;
  top_8 = limit sorted 8;
  generate group as address, top_8.(to) as related_addresses;
}

store top_pairs into '/tmp/related_addresses.txt';
store top_pairs into 'mongodb://localhost/agile_data.related_addresses'
using MongoStorage();
```

Our Flask controller combines several stubs we've already created along with top friends:

```
# Display information about an email address
@app.route('/address/<string:address>')
@app.route('/address/<string:address>/<int:offset1>/<int:offset2>')
def address(address, offset1=0, offset2=config.EMAILS_PER_ADDRESS_PAGE):
  address = address.lower() # In case the email record linking to this isn't
lowered... consider ETL on base document in Pig
  sent_dist = sent_distributions.find_one({'address': address})
  addresses = related_addresses.find_one({'address': address})
   ['related_addresses']
  return render_template('partials/address.html',
                         sent_distribution=sent_dist['sent_distribution'],
                         addresses=addresses,
                         chart_json=json.dumps(sent_dist['sent_distribution']),
                         address='<' + address + '>'
                         )
```

Our template code adds a space for related contacts. Check out *ch07/web/templates/partails/email.html*.

```
{% if addresses -%}
  <h3 style="margin-bottom: 5px;">Email Addresses</h2>
  <ul class="nav nav-pills">
    {% for item in addresses -%}
    <li class="active">
      <a style="margin: 3px;" href="/address/{{ item['address']
         }}">{{ item['address'] }}</a>
```

```
    </li>
    {% endfor -%}
  </ul>
{% endif -%}
```

The results are shown in Figure 7-2.

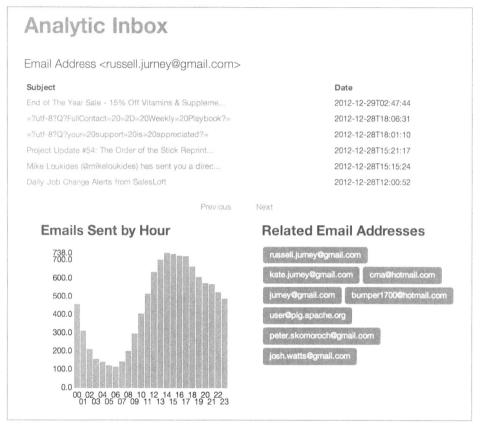

Figure 7-2. Email address page

Linking Records

Having created a report, adding interactivity is easy. Note how we inserted links between email address entities in the preceding section.

We can now explore email addresses and their time habits endlessly! Big deal, right? Maybe not, but it is a good start. Let's extend this by making email addresses in email clickable. We need only extend our macros to add links when displaying email addresses. Check out *ch07/web/templates/macros.jnj*.

```
{% macro limit_length(value, length) -%}
  {% if value|length > 3 -%}{{value|truncate(length=length, killwords=True)}}
  {% endif -%}
{% endmacro -%}

{% macro display_email_address(email_record) -%}
  {% if email_record['real_name'] and email_record['real_name']
  |length > 1 -%}
    {{ display_link(email_record['address']|safe, '/address'|safe,
    limit_length(email_record['real_name'],20)|safe + ' <' + email_record
    ['address']|safe + '>')|safe}}
  {% else -%}
    {{ display_link(email_record['address']|safe, '/address'|safe,
    '<' + email_record['address'] + '>'|safe) }}
  {% endif -%}
{% endmacro -%}
```

Now we can look at email addresses, their properties, and their relationships as we view emails (Figure 7-3). This kind of pivot offers insight, and is a form of simple recommendation.

What we're doing can be described as creating interactive ontologies of semistructured data. Breaking up our process around building this kind of structure does several things for us. First, it creates small batches of work—one per entity—that break efficiently into an agile sprint. This enables a kind of data agility, and also extends our application into a more and more browsable state. This in turn enables users to click around and explore your dataset, which connects the team into the ground truth or reality of the data—which, as you know by now—is a theme in Agile Big Data.

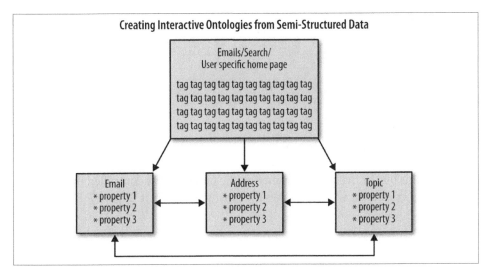

Figure 7-3. Page structure

But we've got a bug (Figure 7-4). For sparse entries, we are skipping hours in our table and chart.

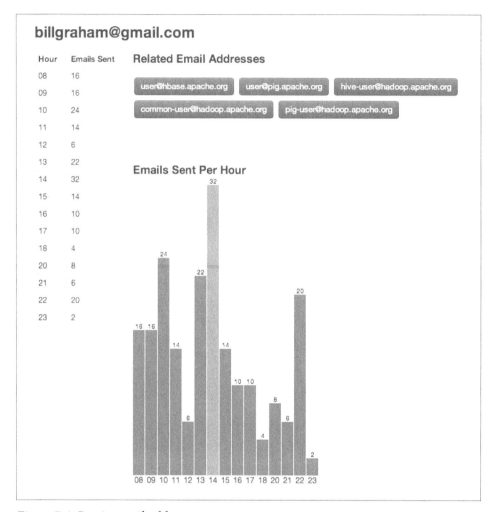

Figure 7-4. Bug in email address page

We can fix this bug in five places: JavaScript, the template, the controller, the database, or with Pig. Let's look at where it makes the most sense to fix it (Figure 7-5).

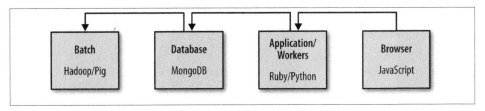

Figure 7-5. Fixing a bug at each level of our stack

```javascript
// Get "00" - "23"
function makeHourRange(num) {
  return num < 10 ? "0" + num.toString() : num.toString();
}

function fillBlanks(rawData) {
  var hourRange = d3.range(0,24);
  var ourData = Array();
  for (hour in hourRange)
  {
    var hourString = makeHourRange(hour);
    var found = false;
    for(x in rawData)
    {
      if(rawData[x]['sent_hour'] == hourString)
      {
        found = true;
        break;
      }
    }
    if(found == true)
    {
      ourData.push(rawData[x]);
    }
    else
    {
      ourData.push({'sent_hour': hourString, 'total': 0})
    }
  }
  return ourData;
}

var rawData = {{ chart_json|safe }};
var filledData = fillBlanks(rawData);
```

First, we can fix the bug in JavaScript in the user's browser. Check out *ch07/web/ templates/partials/address.html.*

It's possible to fix this in the template language, but embedding this kind of logic here is discouraged. Jinja2 isn't for data processing; we can do that elsewhere. Instead, we can fix it in our Python controller by reformatting the data at each request. Check out *ch07/python/sent_distribution_fix.py.*

```python
def fill_in_blanks(in_data):
    out_data = list()
    hours = [ '%02d' % i for i in range(24) ]
    for hour in hours:
        entry = [x for x in in_data if x['sent_hour'] == hour]
        if entry:
            out_data.append(entry[0])
        else:
            out_data.append({'sent_hour': hour, 'total': 0})
    return out_data
```

Changing one line in our controller gets our empty values filled in.

```python
def address(email_address):
    chart_json = json.dumps(fill_in_blanks(sent_dist['sent_dist']))
```

We can see that when it comes to data, Python has teeth. List comprehensions make this implementation fairly succinct.

The problem here is that we're reformatting the data at each request that we formatted ourselves in our Pig script. Why not simply get the format right the first time? Consistency between model and view creates clarity for everyone.

Mongo can use the same JavaScript we used in the web page to fill in empty values in a query. Beautiful, right? There is one exception: we must create our own range() function, as d3.js is not available to MongoDB.

Thanks to the example at *http://stackoverflow.com/questions/8273047/javascript-function-similar-to-python-range*, we can write our own:

```javascript
function range(start, stop, step){
    if (typeof stop=='undefined'){
        // one param defined
        stop = start;
        start = 0;
    };
    if (typeof step=='undefined'){
        step = 1;
    };
    if ((step>0 && start>=stop) || (step<0 && start<=stop)){
        return [];
    };
    var result = [];
    for (var i=start; step>0 ? i<stop : i>stop; i+=step){
        result.push(i);
    };
    return result;
};

// Get "00" - "23"
```

```
function makeHourRange(num) {
  return num < 10 ? "0" + num.toString() : num.toString();
}

function fillBlanks(rawData) {
  var hourRange = range(0,24);
  var ourData = Array();
  for (hour in hourRange)
  {
    var hourString = makeHourRange(hour);
    var found = false;
    for(x in rawData)
    {
      if(rawData[x]['sent_hour'] == hourString)
      {
        found = true;
        break;
      }
    }
    if(found == true)
    {
      ourData.push(rawData[x]);
    }
    else
    {
      ourData.push({'sent_hour': hourString, 'total': 0})
    }
  }
  return ourData;
}

fillBlanks(data);
```

While being able to query our database in JavaScript is convenient, ideally we'd fix the problem at its source. To do so, we can reuse our Python code by modifying it into a Python UDF for Pig and calling this from our script. *Note that Pig converts Pig tuples to tuples and Pig bags to lists of tuples.*

```
@outputSchema("sent_dist:bag{t:(sent_hour:chararray, total:int)}")
def fill_in_blanks(sent_dist):
    print sent_dist
    out_data = list()
    hours = [ '%02d' % i for i in range(24) ]
    for hour in hours:
        entry = [x for x in sent_dist if x[0] == hour]
        if entry:
            entry = entry[0]
            print entry.__class__
            out_data.append(tuple([entry[0], entry[1]]))
        else:
            out_data.append(tuple([hour, 0]))
    return out_data
```

```
/* Load our Jython UDFs */
register 'udfs.py' using jython as funcs;

emails = load '/me/tmp/thu_emails/' using AvroStorage();

...

/* Here we apply our Jython UDF, fill_in_blanks() to fill holes in our time
series. */
filled_dist = foreach sent_distributions generate email, funcs.fill_in_blanks
(sent_dist) as sent_dist;

store filled_dist into '/tmp/filled_distributions.avro' using AvroStorage();
store filled_dist into 'mongodb://localhost/agile_data.sent_dist' using
MongoStorage();
```

We've fixed one bug four different ways (Figure 7-6). In practice we might process data at any part of the stack, but prudence tells us to push our processing deeper in the stack in order to reach a simple, globally consistent view of our entities and their relationships.

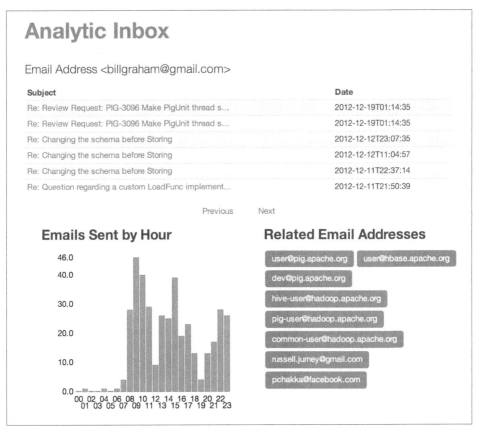

Figure 7-6. Fixed bug

Extracting Keywords from Emails with TF-IDF

Let's get a little bit more sophisticated and tease some structured data from unstructured fields of our semistruttured email documents. To do this, we'll use a derivative of a popular algorithm, TF-IDF (Term Frequency, Inverse Document Frequency), called Normalized Term Frequency, Inverse Document Frequency. TF-IDF works on the principle that words in a document that are common in all documents aren't likely to be as important as words that appear in a document and don't often appear in other documents.

I've implemented this algorithm as a macro. Check out *ch07/pig/ntfidf.macro*.

```
# Derived from TF-IDF by Jacob Perkins at
http://thedatachef.blogspot.com/2011/04/tf-idf-with-apache-pig.html with
# help from Mat Kelcey who referred me to
http://nlp.stanford.edu/IR-book/html/htmledition/maximum-tf-normalization-1.html
```

```
/* A Pig Macro to implement the NTF-IDF Algorithm */
DEFINE ntf_idf(token_records, id_field, token_field) RETURNS out_relation {

  /* Calculate the term count per document */
  doc_word_totals = foreach (group $token_records by ($id_field, $token_field))
  generate
    FLATTEN(group) as ($id_field, token),
    COUNT_STAR($token_records) as doc_total;

  /* Calculate the document size */
  pre_term_counts = foreach (group doc_word_totals by $id_field) generate
    group AS $id_field,
    FLATTEN(doc_word_totals.(token, doc_total)) as (token, doc_total),
    SUM(doc_word_totals.doc_total) as doc_size,
    MAX(doc_word_totals.doc_total) as max_freq;

  /* Calculate the TF - Term Frequency */
  term_freqs = foreach pre_term_counts generate
    $id_field as $id_field,
    token as token,
    ((double)doc_total / (double)doc_size / (double) max_freq) AS term_freq;

  /* Get count of documents using each token, for idf */
  token_usages = foreach (group term_freqs by token) generate
    FLATTEN(term_freqs) as ($id_field:chararray, token:chararray,
    term_freq:double),
    COUNT_STAR(term_freqs) as num_docs_with_token;

  /* Get document count */
  just_ids = foreach $token_records generate $id_field;
  just_ids = DISTINCT just_ids;
  ndocs = foreach (group just_ids all) generate COUNT_STAR(just_ids)
  as total_docs;

  /* Note the use of Pig Scalars to calculate idf */
  scores = foreach token_usages {
    idf    = LOG((double)ndocs.total_docs/(double)num_docs_with_token);
    ntf_idf = (double)term_freq * idf;
    generate $id_field as $id_field,
      token as token,
      (double)ntf_idf as score:double;
  };

  $out_relation = filter scores by token IS NOT NULL and token != ''
  and LENGTH(token) > 2; -- score > 0.10 and
};
```

This is called by *ch07/pig/topics.pig*. Note that this script uses the TokenizeText UDF from the varaha project, which is available at *https://github.com/Ganglion/varaha*. To install varaha, run:

```
git clone git@github.com:Ganglion/varaha.git
cd varaha
mvn install
```

The script itself is straightforward:

```
/* Set Home Directory - where we install software */
%default HOME `echo \$HOME/Software/`

/* Avro uses json-simple, and is in piggybank until Pig 0.12, where AvroStorage and
TrevniStorage are builtins */
REGISTER $HOME/pig/build/ivy/lib/Pig/avro-1.5.3.jar
REGISTER $HOME/pig/build/ivy/lib/Pig/json-simple-1.1.jar
REGISTER $HOME/pig/contrib/piggybank/java/piggybank.jar

DEFINE AvroStorage org.apache.pig.piggybank.storage.avro.AvroStorage();
DEFINE LENGTH org.apache.pig.piggybank.evaluation.string.LENGTH();

REGISTER $HOME/varaha/lib/*.jar /* Varaha has a good tokenizer */
REGISTER $HOME/varaha/target/varaha-1.0-SNAPSHOT.jar

DEFINE TokenizeText varaha.text.TokenizeText();

set default_parallel 20

rmf /tmp/tf_idf_scores.txt
rmf /tmp/ntf_idf_scores.txt
rmf /tmp/trimmed_tokens.txt

register 'udfs.py' using jython as funcs;
import 'ntfidf.macro';

/* Load emails and trim unneeded fields */
emails = load '/me/Data/test_mbox' using AvroStorage();
id_body_address = foreach emails generate message_id, body, from.address as
address;

/* Project and flatten to message_id/address/token and basic filter */
token_records_address = foreach id_body_address generate message_id, address,
FLATTEN(TokenizeText(body)) as token;
trimmed_tokens = filter token_records_address by token is not null and token
!= '' and LENGTH(token) > 2;
store trimmed_tokens into '/tmp/trimmed_tokens.txt';

/* Run topics per message */
ntf_idf_scores_per_message = ntf_idf(trimmed_tokens, 'message_id', 'token');
store ntf_idf_scores_per_message into '/tmp/ntf_idf_scores_per_message.txt';
```

Once topics per document and their scores are calculated, they are processed into groups per document, with the top *N* topics for the document in each group. Check out *ch07/ pig/process_topics.pig.*

```
set default_parallel 20

rmf /tmp/topics_per_document.txt

-- Topics Per Document
topic_scores_per_message = LOAD '/tmp/ntf_idf_scores_per_message.txt' as
(message_id:chararray, topic:chararray, score:double);
per_document = foreach (group topic_scores_per_message by message_id) {
  sorted = order topic_scores_per_message by score desc;
  limited = limit sorted 10;
  generate group as message_id, limited.(topic, score);
};
store per_document into '/tmp/topics_per_document.txt';
```

Finally, the topics are stored in Mongo in the *topics_per_email* relation, by *ch07/pig/ publish_topics_per_email.pig.*

```
/* Set Home Directory - where we install software */
%default HOME `echo \$HOME/Software/`

/* MongoDB libraries and configuration */
REGISTER $HOME/mongo-hadoop/mongo-2.10.1.jar
REGISTER $HOME/mongo-hadoop/core/target/mongo-hadoop-core-1.1.0-SNAPSHOT.jar
REGISTER $HOME/mongo-hadoop/pig/target/mongo-hadoop-pig-1.1.0-SNAPSHOT.jar

DEFINE MongoStorage com.mongodb.hadoop.pig.MongoStorage();

per_document_scores = LOAD '/tmp/topics_per_document.txt' AS
(message_id:chararray, topics:bag{topic:tuple(word:chararray, score:double)});
store per_document_scores into 'mongodb://localhost/agile_data.topics_per_email'
using MongoStorage();
```

Checking on our data in MongoDB yields:

```
db.topics_per_email.findOne()
{
"_id" : ObjectId("510ef2803004df85dba4ec3a"),
"message_id" : "CANSvDjrA-dea9T-iZ6wJOLBP_Kqriae3FMDasU2Ox00gfzxJjg@mail.gmail.com",
"topics" : [
 {
 "word" : "grass",
 "score" : 0.31845143365191986
  },
  {
   "word" : "plant",
   "score" : 0.2810330077326449
  },
  {
   "word" : "rye",
   "score" : 0.20285020154575548
  },
  {
   "word" : "sack",
```

```
    "score" : 0.19571670266698085
  },
  {
   "word" : "topsoil",
   "score" : 0.19381049907089434
  },
  {
   "word" : "warms",
   "score" : 0.19207027153110176
  },
  {
   "word" : "turf",
   "score" : 0.1889872579345566
  },
  {
   "word" : "weeds",
   "score" : 0.16849717160426886
  },
  {
   "word" : "winter",
   "score" : 0.13641124134559518
  },
  {
   "word" : "dad",
   "score" : 0.12483962902570728
  }
 ]
}
```

We display these records in our controller for emails:

```python
# Controller: Fetch an email and display it
@app.route("/email/<message_id>")
def email(message_id):
    email = emails.find_one({'message_id': message_id})
    address_hash = addresses_per_email.find_one({'message_id': message_id})
    sent_dist_records = sent_distributions.find_one({'address': email['from']
    ['address']})
    topics = topics_per_email.find_one({'message_id': message_id})
    return render_template('partials/email.html', email=email,
                                                   addresses=address_hash
                                                   ['addresses'],
                                                   chart_json=json.dumps
                                                   (sent_dist_records
                                                   ['sent_distribution']),
                                                   sent_distribution=
                                                   sent_dist_records,
                                                   topics=topics)
```

In our template:

```html
{% if topics -%}
  <h3 style="margin-bottom: 5px;">Topics</h2>
  <ul class="nav nav-pills">
```

```
    {% for item in topics['topics'] -%}
    <li class="active">
      <a style="margin: 3px;" href="/topic/{{ item['word'] }}">{{ item['word'] }}</a>
    </li>
    {% endfor -%}
  </ul>
{% endif -%}
```

And finally, in our browser, as Figure 7-7 shows.

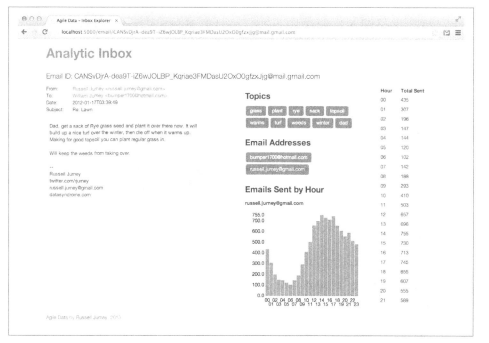

Figure 7-7. Email topics

Conclusion

Here's a summary of what we've done so far in these steps:

1. Create interesting, interconnected records. The bar for "interesting" is initially low. We will improve it over time based on user feedback, traffic analysis, and noodling.

2. Store these records as objects in a document store, like so:

```
key => {property1, property2, links => [key1, key2, key3]}
```

Split records as properties increase and become complex to avoid deep nesting. Or go at it as a document. Both approaches are valid if they fit your data.

3. Use a lightweight web framework like Flask or Sinatra to emit the key/value data as JSON, or use a document store that returns JSON in the first place.

## CHAPTER 8

Making Predictions

Now that we have interactive reports exposing different aspects of our data, we're ready to make our first prediction. This forms our fourth agile sprint (Figure 8-1). When making predictions, we take what we know about the past and project what will happen in the future, simultaneously transitioning from batch processing of historical data to real-time classification of the present to predict the future. We'll start simply, moving on to driving real actions in the next chapter.

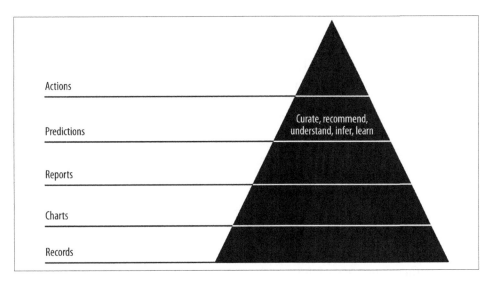

Figure 8-1. Level 4: making predictions

Code examples for this chapter are available at *https://github.com/rjurney/ Agile_Data_Code/tree/master/ch08*. Clone the repository and follow along!

```
git clone https://github.com/rjurney/Agile_Data_Code.git
```

Predicting Response Rates to Emails

When I click around in our application and look at the charts showing how often some-one emails by hour of the day, I wonder if we can infer from this data when someone is most likely to reply. This is why we created charts and reports in the first place—to guide us as we climb the data-value pyramid.

In this chapter, we will predict whether a recipient will respond to a given email using some of the entities we've extracted from our inbox. In the next chapter, we'll use this inference to enable a new kind of action.

We're going to walk from simple frequencies to real insight one table at a time, just as we did in Chapter 2. This time, we'll show you the code to accompany the logic.

We begin by calculating a simple overall sent count between pairs of emails (Figure 8-2). Check out *ch08/p_reply.pig*.

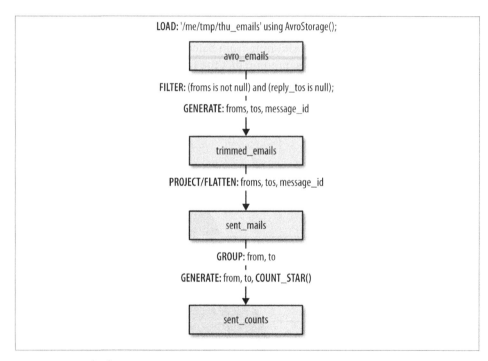

Figure 8-2. Calculating sent counts

```
/* Get rid of emails with reply_to; they confuse everything in mailing lists. */
avro_emails = load '/me/tmp/thu_emails' using AvroStorage();
clean_emails = filter avro_emails by (froms is not null) and (reply_tos is null);

/* Treat emails without in_reply_to as sent emails */
```

```
trimmed_emails = foreach clean_emails generate froms, tos, message_id;
sent_mails = foreach trimmed_emails generate flatten(froms.address) as from,
                                             flatten(tos.address) as to,
                                             message_id;
store sent_counts into '/tmp/sent_counts';
```

Global sent counts between pairs of email addresses are easy enough to calculate, as this is roughly equivalent to a SQL `group by`: we use the `flatten` command to project all unique pairs of *from*/*to* in each email (remember: emails can have more than one *to*), along with the `message_id` of the email. See Table 8-1.

Table 8-1. Sent counts—simple frequencies

From	To	Total
russell.jurney@gmail.com	*****@hotmail.com*	237
russell.jurney@gmail.com	*jurney@gmail.com*	122
russell.jurney@gmail.com	******.jurney@gmail.com*	273

The next step is a little more complex. We need to separate replies. Since we will be using overall sent counts as the denominator in determining our reply ratios, we need to remove all mailing list emails from the analysis. Calculating the sent counts for the entire lurking population of a mailing list is daunting, to say the least!

Our calculation is the same as for total emails, except we filter so that all emails have a nonnull `in_reply_to`, and we project `in_reply_to` with our email pairs instead of `message_id`.

```
/* Remove in_reply_tos, as they are mailing lists which have incalculable total
sent_counts */
avro_emails2 = load '/me/tmp/thu_emails' using AvroStorage();
replies = filter avro_emails2 by (froms is not null) and (reply_tos is null)
and (in_reply_to is not null);
replies = foreach replies generate flatten(froms.address) as from,
                                   flatten(tos.address) as to,
                                   in_reply_to;
replies = filter replies by in_reply_to != 'None';
store replies into '/tmp/replies';
```

 Note that we have to load the emails twice to effect a self-join. As of Pig 0.10, Pig can't join a relation to itself.

We are now prepared to join the sent messages with the replies to see each email and whether it was replied to at all (Figure 8-3).

```
/* Now join a copy of the emails by message id to the in_reply_to of our emails */
with_reply = join sent_mails by message_id, replies by in_reply_to;
```

```
/* Filter out mailing lists - only direct replies where from/to match up */
direct_replies = filter with_reply by (sent_mails::from == replies::to) and
(sent_mails::to == replies::from);
store direct_replies into '/tmp/direct_replies';
```

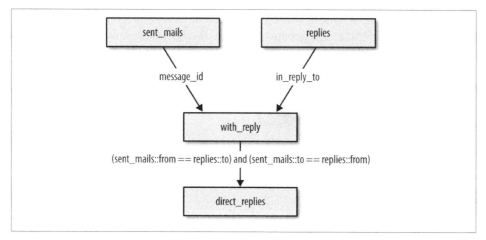

Figure 8-3. Self-join of emails with replies

The data at this point looks like the following. Notice how we've used a join (in this case, a self-join) to filter our data, which is a pattern in dataflow programming with Pig.

```
from  to  message_id  from  to  in_reply_to
russell.jurney@gmail.com kate.jurney@gmail.com
CANSvDjrAR+ZHnxES3hBUZV+wJY_0ZbhzH0wjJEmiCTzBQGH10Q@mail.gmail.com
    kate.jurney@gmail.com russell.jurney@gmail.com
CANSvDjrAR+ZHnxES3hBUZV+wJY_0ZbhzH0wjJEmiCTzBQGH10Q@mail.gmail.com
russell.jurney@gmail.com kate.jurney@gmail.com
CANSvDjrLdcnk7_bPk-pLK2dSDF9Hw_6YScespnEnrnAEY8hocw@mail.gmail.com
    kate.jurney@gmail.com russell.jurney@gmail.com
CANSvDjrLdcnk7_bPk-pLK2dSDF9Hw_6YScespnEnrnAEY8hocw@mail.gmail.com
russell.jurney@gmail.com kate.jurney@gmail.com
CANSvDjrX00pOC53j7B=sm4TMyTUVpG_GWxT-cUi=MtrGDDcs1Q@mail.gmail.com
    kate.jurney@gmail.com russell.jurney@gmail.com
CANSvDjrX00pOC53j7B=sm4TMyTUVpG_GWxT-cUi=MtrGDDcs1Q@mail.gmail.com
russell.jurney@gmail.com kate.jurney@gmail.com
CANSvDjrbuxc4ik3PPAy9OcRf3au9ww3ivkFKv8rwwdEsqvAAMw@mail.gmail.com
    kate.jurney@gmail.com russell.jurney@gmail.com
CANSvDjrbuxc4ik3PPAy9OcRf3au9ww3ivkFKv8rwwdEsqvAAMw@mail.gmail.com
```

Since we have duplicate fields after the join, we can drop them:

```
direct_replies = foreach direct_replies generate sent_mails::from as from,
sent_mails::to as to;
```

The semantics of our data are now, "The message from A to B with ID C was replied to, from B to A."

```
from  to  message_id
russell.jurney@gmail.com  kate.jurney@gmail.com  CANSvDjrAR+ZHnxE0Z…@mail.gmail.com
russell.jurney@gmail.com  kate.jurney@gmail.com  CANSvDjrL+2dSDF9Hw…@mail.gmail.com
russell.jurney@gmail.com  kate.jurney@gmail.com  CANSvDjrXO0p=sTUVp…@mail.gmail.com
russell.jurney@gmail.com  kate.jurney@gmail.com  CANSvDjrbuxc4iau9w…@mail.gmail.com
```

Now we're ready to calculate reply counts between pairs of email addresses (Table 8-2).

```
reply_counts = foreach(group direct_replies by (from, to)) generate flatten(group)
as (from, to),
                                    COUNT_STAR(direct_replies) as total;
store reply_counts into '/tmp/reply_counts';
```

Table 8-2. Reply counts

From	To	Total replies
russell.jurney@gmail.com	****@hotmail.com	60
russell.jurney@gmail.com	jurney@gmail.com	31
russell.jurney@gmail.com	****.jurney@gmail.com	36

Having calculated total emails sent between email addresses, as well as the number of replies, we can calculate reply ratios: how often one email address replies to another (see Figure 8-4 and Table 8-3).

```
sent_replies = join sent_counts by (from, to), reply_counts by (from, to);
reply_ratios = foreach sent_replies generate sent_counts::from as from,
                                    sent_counts::to as to,
                                    (float)reply_counts::total/(float)
                                    sent_counts::total as ratio;
reply_ratios = foreach reply_ratios generate from, to, (ratio > 1.0 ? 1.0 :
ratio) as ratio;
```

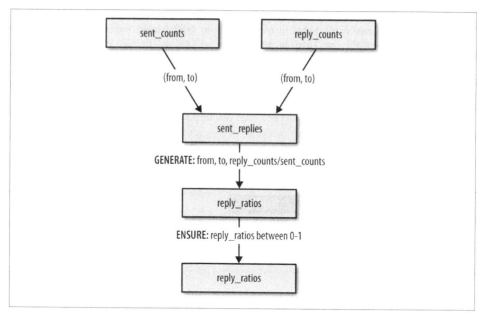

Figure 8-4. Calculating reply ratios

Table 8-3. P(response|email)

From	To	P(response|email)
russell.jurney@gmail.com	*****@hotmail.com*	0.25316456
russell.jurney@gmail.com	*jurney@gmail.com*	0.25409836
russell.jurney@gmail.com	****.jurney@gmail.com*	0.13186814

What this means is that given an email from *russel.jurney@gmail.com* to *****@gmail.com*, we can expect 0.25 replies. Another way of saying this is that there is a reply about 25% of the time.

Finally, we publish this data to MongoDB and verify that it arrived.

```
store reply_ratios into 'mongodb://localhost/agile_data.reply_ratios'
using MongoStorage();

> db.reply_ratios.findOne({"from": "russell.jurney@gmail.com", "to":
"kate.jurney@gmail.com"})
{
  "_id" : ObjectId("5010f7df0364e16aa73da639"),
  "from" : "russell.jurney@gmail.com",
  "to" : "kate.jurney@gmail.com",
  "ratio" : 0.1318681389093399
}
```

Now let's add this feature to our email address page.

Personalization

Up to now we've made no assumptions about the user of our application. That is about to change. In this section we will assume the user is me: *russell.jurney@gmail.com*. In practice, we would authorize and log in a user and then import and present data from his perspective via a unique session. To simplify the examples, we'll just assume we're me.

Insert a fetch for `reply_ratio` into our Flask app:

```
reply_ratio = db.reply_ratios.find_one({'from': 'russell.jurney@gmail.com',
'to': email_address})
  return render_template('partials/address.html', reply_ratio=reply_ratio, ...
```

Edit our template for the address page to display the value (Figure 8-5). Note that we've skipped displaying each step in our calculation. As you become more comfortable with your dataset, you can chunk in larger batches. Still, it is a good idea to publish frequently to keep everyone on the team on the same page, and to give everyone access to building blocks to create new features from.

```
<div class="span6" style="margin-top: 25px">
  <h3>Probability of Reply</h3>
  <p style="white-space:nowrap;">{{ reply_ratio['from']}}  ->  {{
    reply_ratio['to']}}:   {{
  reply_ratio['ratio']|round(2) }}</p>
</div>
```

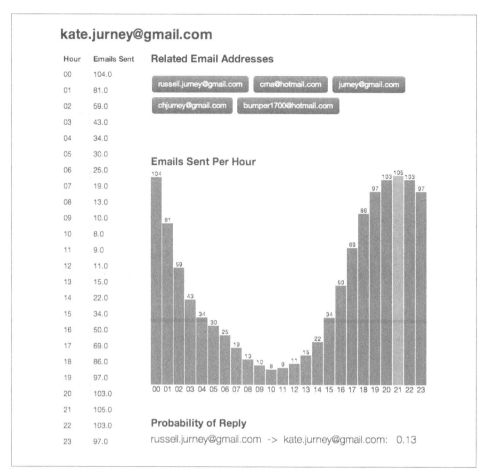

Figure 8-5. Displaying reply ratio

Conclusion

In this chapter we've taken what we know about the past to predict the future. We now know the odds that an email we are sending will be replied to. This can guide us in whom we email—after all, if we are expecting a response, we might not bother to email someone who doesn't reply!

In the next chapter, we'll drill down into this prediction to drive a new action that can take advantage of it.

## CHAPTER 9

Driving Actions

In this chapter, our fifth and final agile sprint, we will translate predictions into action by diving further into what makes an email likely or not to elicit a response and turning this into an interactive feature (Figure 9-1). We'll learn to suggest changes to email authors that will make their emails better.

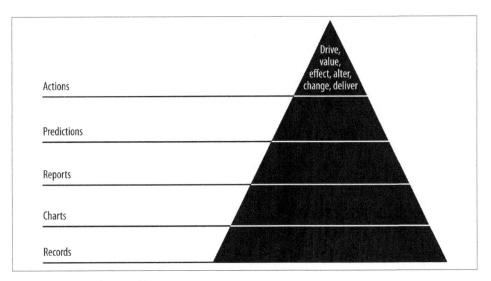

Figure 9-1. Level 5: enabling action

Up to now we've created charts associated with entities we've extracted from our emails, built entity pages that link together to form reports for interactive exploration of our data, and calculated probabilities that help us reason about the future to tell whether we can likely expect a response to an email.

This poses an opportunity to dig further. We've found a lever with which we can drive actions: predicting whether an email will receive a response. If we can increase the odds of a response, we've enabled a valuable action.

With driving actions—the improvement of emails—we have arrived at the final stage of the data-value pyramid: enabling new actions.

```
git clone https://github.com/rjurney/Agile_Data_Code.git
```

Properties of Successful Emails

We've already seen that the time of day has a large effect on email: people send more emails at certain times of day, and we might infer that they also reply more to emails at that time. Email is, after all, a stack, and the most recent emails are those at the top of the stack most likely to grab our attention.

We'll use our intuition to come up with some more factors that might affect reply rates. In this chapter, we'll go from a single conditional probability implying a prediction to multiple probabilities combined to make a real prediction about user behavior. We'll plug this prediction into an API callable in real time, using what we've learned about the past to predict the future in the present.

Better Predictions with Naive Bayes

We can do better than employ single conditional probabilities to predict the future. We can combine more than one kind of evidence to get better accuracy in our prediction. For instance, we have computed the probability that a given email address will reply, but doesn't the content of the message also matter? We'd like to think so. We can reason about our problem domain to think this through.

How might we figure out whether a user replies to emails at the top of the stack? Well, let's look at the signals we've already prepared: Who emails whom and how often? What about email topics? We could determine similarity between emails and then, more important, who replies about what?

P(Reply | From & To)

In the previous chapter, we calculated *P(reply | from & to)*, or "the probability of reply, given *from* and *to* email addresses," and we displayed it in our application as a simple prediction. We'll continue to use this meaningful data in our real-time prediction making, combining it with another factor to achieve a more accurate prediction.

To calculate *P(reply | from & to)*, check out *ch09/pig/p_reply_given_from_to.pig* and run `cd pig; pig -l /tmp -x local -v -w p_reply_given_from_to.pig`.

Its contents will look familiar from the previous chapter.

P(Reply | Token)

Email bodies are rich in signal. Having extracted topics, what if we use the same kind of processing and associate the tokens with messages and replies to determine the probability of a reply for each token? Then, in combination, if we combine the reply probability of all tokens, we'll have a good idea of a message's chance of getting a reply in terms of its content.

Check out *ch09/pig/p_reply_given_topics.pig*. We load emails as usual, then trim them to message_id/body as an optimization. We don't need the extra fields.

```
emails = load '/me/Data/test_mbox' using AvroStorage();
id_body = foreach emails generate message_id, body;
```

Next, we get counts for each token's appearance in each document:

```
/* Tokenize text, count of each token per document */
token_records = foreach id_body generate message_id, FLATTEN(TokenizeText(body))
as token;
doc_word_totals = foreach (group token_records by (message_id, token)) generate
  FLATTEN(group) as (message_id, token),
  COUNT_STAR(token_records) as doc_total;
```

Then we calculate document size to normalize these token counts:

```
/* Calculate the document size */
pre_term_counts = foreach (group doc_word_totals by message_id) generate
  group AS message_id,
  FLATTEN(doc_word_totals.(token, doc_total)) as (token, doc_total),
  SUM(doc_word_totals.doc_total) as doc_size;
```

Next, we divide token counts by document size to normalize them.

```
/* Calculate the Term Frequency */
term_freqs = foreach pre_term_counts generate
  message_id as message_id,
  token as token,
  ((double)doc_total / (double)doc_size) AS term_freq;
```

Finally, calculate the number of times a token has been sent, or used, overall in all emails in our corpus (inbox):

```
/* By Term - Calculate the SENT COUNT */
total_term_freqs = foreach (group term_freqs by token) generate
(chararray)group as token,
SUM(term_freqs.term_freq) as total_freq_sent;
```

Having calculated the frequencies for each token across our entire corpus, we now need to calculate the number of replies to these same emails. To do that, we trim emails down

to message_id and in_reply_to as an optimization, and then join the replies by in_re
ply_to with the sent emails by message_id.

```
replies = foreach emails generate message_id, in_reply_to;
with_replies = join term_freqs by message_id LEFT OUTER, replies by in_reply_to;
```

Having joined our replies with a LEFT OUTER, we have a relation that contains emails
that were replied to, and those that weren't. Now we need to split the data off into parallel
computations for two paths: the chance of reply, and the chance of not replying.

```
/* Split, because we're going to calculate P(reply|token) and P(no reply|token) */
split with_replies into has_reply if (in_reply_to is not null), no_reply if
(in_reply_to is null);
```

Now for each split, we calculate the probability of a reply/not reply occurring, starting
with the sum of uses per token:

```
total_replies = foreach (group with_replies by term_freqs::token) generate
(chararray)group as token,
    SUM(with_replies.term_freqs::term_freq) as total_freq_replied;
```

Finally, we join our overall sent-token counts and the associated reply counts to get our
answer, the probability of reply for each token.

```
    sent_totals_reply_totals = JOIN total_term_freqs by token, total_replies by token;
token_reply_rates = foreach sent_totals_reply_totals
generate total_term_freqs::token as token, (double)total_freq_replied /
(double)total_freq_sent as reply_rate;
store token_reply_rates into '/tmp/reply_rates.txt';
```

Now, to publish our result, check out *ch09/pig/publish_topics.pig*. It is simple enough:

```
/* MongoDB libraries and configuration */
REGISTER /me/Software/mongo-hadoop/mongo-2.10.1.jar
REGISTER /me/Software/mongo-hadoop/core/target/
mongo-hadoop-core-1.1.0-SNAPSHOT.jar
REGISTER /me/Software/mongo-hadoop/pig/target/
mongo-hadoop-pig-1.1.0-SNAPSHOT.jar

DEFINE MongoStorage com.mongodb.hadoop.pig.MongoStorage();

token_reply_rates = LOAD '/tmp/reply_rates.txt' AS
(token:chararray, reply_rate:double);
store token_reply_rates into 'mongodb://localhost/agile_data.token_reply_rates'
using MongoStorage();

token_no_reply_rates = LOAD '/tmp/no_reply_rates.txt' AS
(token:chararray, reply_rate:double);
store token_no_reply_rates into 'mongodb://localhost/
agile_data.token_no_reply_rates' using MongoStorage();

p_token = LOAD '/tmp/p_token.txt' AS (token:chararray, prob:double);
store p_token into 'mongodb://localhost/agile_data.p_token' using MongoStorage();
```

Check our topics in MongoDB. Check out *https://github.com/rjurney/Agile_Data_Code/blob/master/ch09/mongo.js*. From Mongo, run:

```
db.token_reply_rates.ensureIndex({token: 1})

db.token_reply_rates.findOne({token:'public'})
{
  "_id" : ObjectId("511700c330048b60597e7c04"),
  "token" : "public",
  "reply_rate" : 0.6969366812896153
}
db.token_no_reply_rates.findOne({'token': 'public'})
{
  "_id" : ObjectId("518444d83004f7fadcb48b51"),
  "token" : "public",
  "reply_rate" : 0.4978798266965859
}
```

Our next step is to use these probabilities to go real-time with a prediction!

Making Predictions in Real Time

We analyze the past to understand trends that inform us about the future. We employ that data in real time to make predictions. In this section, we'll use both data sources we've predicted in combination to make predictions in real time, in response to HTTP requests.

Check out *ch09/classify.py*. This is a simple web application that takes three arguments: *from* email address, *to* email address, and the message body, and returns whether the email will receive a reply or not.

We begin importing Flask and pymongo as usual, but we'll also be using NLTK (*http://nltk.org/*) (the Python Natural Language Toolkit). NLTK sets the standard in open source, natural language processing. There is an excellent book on NLTK, available here: *http://nltk.org/book/*. We'll be using the NLTK utility word_tokenize.

```
import pymongo
from flask import Flask, request
from nltk.tokenize import word_tokenize
```

Next, we set up MongoDB to call on our probability tables for from/to and tokens:

```
conn = pymongo.Connection() # defaults to localhost
db = conn.agile_data
from_to_reply_ratios = db['from_to_reply_ratios']
from_to_no_reply_ratios = db['from_to_no_reply_ratios']
p_sent_from_to = db['p_sent_from_to']
token_reply_rates = db['token_reply_rates']
token_no_reply_rates = db['token_no_reply_rates']
p_token = db['p_token']
```

Our controller starts simply, at the URL */will_reply*. We get the arguments to the URL, *from*, *to*, and *body*:

```
app = Flask(__name__)

# Controller: Fetch an email and display it
@app.route("/will_reply")
def will_reply():

# Get the message_id, from, first to, and message body
message_id = request.args.get('mesage_id')
from = request.args.get('from')
to = request.args.get('to')
body = request.args.get('message_body')
```

Next we process the tokens in the message body for both cases, reply and no-reply:

```
# For each token in the body, if there's a match in MongoDB,
  # append it and average all of them at the end
  reply_probs = []
  reply_rate = 1
  no_reply_probs = []
  no_reply_rate = 1
  if(body):
    for token in word_tokenize(body):

      prior = p_token.find_one({'token': token}) # db.p_token.ensureIndex
      ({'token': 1})
      reply_search = token_reply_rates.find_one({'token': token}) #
      db.token_reply_rates.ensureIndex({'token': 1})
      no_reply_search = token_no_reply_rates.find_one({'token': token}) #
      db.token_no_reply_rates.ensureIndex({'token': 1})
      if reply_search:
        word_prob = reply_search['reply_rate'] * prior['prob']
        print("Token: " + token + " Reply Prob: " + str(word_prob))
        reply_probs.append(word_prob)
      if no_reply_search:
        word_prob = no_reply_search['reply_rate'] * prior['prob']
        print("Token: " + token + " No Reply Prob: " + str(word_prob))
        no_reply_probs.append(word_prob)
  reply_ary = float(len(reply_probs))
  reply_rate = sum(reply_probs) / (len(reply_probs) if len(reply_probs)
  > 0 else 1)
  no_reply_ary = float(len(no_reply_probs))
  no_reply_rate = sum(no_reply_probs) / (len(no_reply_probs) if
  len(no_reply_probs) > 0 else 1)
```

Look what's happening: we tokenize the body into a list of words using NLTK, and then look up the reply probability of each word in MongoDB. We append these reply probabilities to a list, and then take the average of the list.

Next, we do the same for from/to:

```
# Use from/to probabilities when available
ftrr = from_to_reply_ratios.find_one({'from': froms, 'to': to}) #
  db.from_to_reply_ratios.ensureIndex({from: 1, to: 1})
ftnrr = from_to_no_reply_ratios.find_one({'from': froms, 'to': to}) #
  db.from_to_no_reply_ratios.ensureIndex({from: 1, to: 1})
if ftrr:
  p_from_to_reply = ftrr['ratio']
  p_from_to_no_reply = ftnrr['ratio']
else:
  p_from_to_reply = 1.0
  p_from_to_no_reply = 1.0
```

If the from/to reply probabilities aren't available, we use a placeholder. Finally, we evaluate the probabilities for reply and no-reply and take the larger one.

```
# Combine the two predictions
positive = reply_rate * p_from_to_reply
negative = no_reply_rate * p_from_to_no_reply
print "%2f vs %2f" % (positive, negative)
result = "REPLY" if positive > negative else "NO REPLY"

return render_template('partials/will_reply.html', result=result, froms=froms,
to=to, message_body=body)
```

Our template is simple:

```
<!-- Extend our site layout -->
{% extends "layout.html" %}

<!-- Include our common macro set -->
{% import "macros.jnj" as common %}

{% block content -%}

<form action="/will_reply" method="get">
  <fieldset>
  <label>From:</label>
  <input type="text" name="from" value="{{ froms }}"></input>
  <label>To:</label>
  <input type="text" name="to" value="{{ to }}"></input>
  <label>Body:</label>
  <textarea rows="4" name="message_body" style="width: 500px">{{ message_body }}
  </textarea>
  </fieldset>
  <button type="submit" class="btn">Submit</button>
</form>

<p>{{ result }}</p>

{% endblock -%}
```

And we'll need to add a few indexes to make the queries performant:

```
db.p_token.ensureIndex({'token': 1})
db.token_reply_rates.ensureIndex({'token': 1})
db.token_no_reply_rates.ensureIndex({'token': 1})
db.from_to_reply_ratios.ensureIndex({from: 1, to: 1})
db.from_to_no_reply_ratios.ensureIndex({from: 1, to: 1})
```

Run the application with python ./index.py and then visit /will_reply and enter values that will work for your inbox (Figure 9-2).

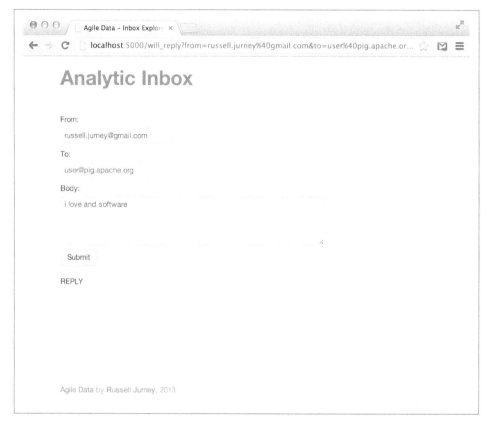

Figure 9-2. Will reply UI

Wheeeee! It's fun to see what different content does to the chance of reply, isn't it?

Logging Events

We've come full circle—from collecting to analyzing events, inferring things about the future, and then serving these insights up in real time. Now our application is generating logs that are new events, and the data cycle closes:

```
127.0.0.1 - - [10/Feb/2013 20:50:32] "GET /favicon.ico HTTP/1.1" 404 -
    {u'to': u'**@****.com.com', u'_id': ObjectId('5111f1cd30043dc319d96141'),
    u'from': u'russell.jurney@gmail.com', u'ratio': 0.54}
    127.0.0.1 - - [10/Feb/2013 20:50:39] "GET /will_reply/?
    from=russell.jurney@gmail.com&to=**@****.com.com&body=startup HTTP/1.1" 200 -
    127.0.0.1 - - [10/Feb/2013 20:50:40] "GET /favicon.ico HTTP/1.1" 404 -
    {u'to': u'**@****.com.com', u'_id': ObjectId('5111f1cd30043dc319d96141'),
    u'from': u'russell.jurney@gmail.com', u'ratio': 0.54}
    127.0.0.1 - - [10/Feb/2013 20:50:45] "GET /will_reply/?
    from=russell.jurney@gmail.com&to=**@****.com.com&body=startup HTTP/1.1" 200 -
    {u'to': u'**@****.com.com', u'_id': ObjectId('5111f1cd30043dc319d96141'),
    u'from': u'russell.jurney@gmail.com', u'ratio': 0.54}
    127.0.0.1 - - [10/Feb/2013 20:51:04] "GET /will_reply/?
    from=russell.jurney@gmail.com&to=**@****.com.com&body=i%20work%20at%20a
    %20hadoop%20startup HTTP/1.1" 200 -
    127.0.0.1 - - [10/Feb/2013 20:51:04] "GET /favicon.ico HTTP/1.1" 404 -
    {u'to': u'**@****.com.com', u'_id': ObjectId('5111f1cd30043dc319d96141'),
    u'from': u'russell.jurney@gmail.com', u'ratio': 0.54}
    127.0.0.1 - - [10/Feb/2013 20:51:08] "GET /will_reply/?
    from=russell.jurney@gmail.com&to=**@****.com.com&body=i%20work%20at%20a
    %20hadoop%20startup HTTP/1.1" 200 -
```

We might log these events and include them in our analysis to further refine our application. In any case, having satisfied our mission to enable new actions, we've come to a close. We can now run our emails through this filter to understand how likely we are to receive a reply and change the emails accordingly.

Conclusion

In this chapter, we have created a prediction service that helps to drive an action: enabling better emails by predicting whether a response will occur. This is the highest level of the data-value pyramid, and it brings this book to a close. We've come full circle from creating simple document pages to making real-time predictions.

Index

We'd like to hear your suggestions for improving our indexes. Send email to index@oreilly.com.

structured data, 18
SUBSTR function (MySQL), 20

T

tables, defining, 20–23
Taiwo, Akinyele Samuel, 13
teams
    adapting to change, 8–10
    Agile Big Data process, 11
    code review, 12
    engineering productivity, 13
    pair programming, 12
    recognizing opportunities and problems, 6–
       8
    roles within, 5
templates, Jinja2, 94–98, 118
Term Frequency, Inverse Document Frequency
    (TF-IDF), 133–138
testing Python Avro client, 40
TF-IDF (Term Frequency, Inverse Document
    Frequency), 133–138
Thrift serialization system, 24
time series (timestamps) perspective, 30
time, visualizing, 116–122
TokenizeText UDF, 134
Torvalds, Linus, 67
Tschetter, Eric, 5

U

UDFs (user-defined functions), 82, 131, 134
universally unique identifier (UUID), 25
user experience designers (team role), 6–10

user-defined functions (UDFs), 82, 131, 134
UUID (universally unique identifier), 25

V

varaha project, 134
venv (virtual environment), 39
virtualenv package (Python), 39
visualizing data
    about, 63
    with charts, 111–122
    visualizing time, 116–122

W

Warden, Pete, 25
waterfall method, 4
web applications
    about, 39
    lightweight, 56–58
web developers (team role), 6–10
Wonderdog interface (Hadoop), 53–55, 106
word frequency counts, 32
word_tokenize utility, 153
workflows
    Agile Big Data processing, 38
    Elastic MapReduce, 72–76
    expert contributor, 6–8
    lightweight web applications, 56–58

Y

YAGNI principle, 26

About the Author

Russell Jurney cut his data teeth in casino gaming, building web apps to analyze the performance of slot machines in the US and Mexico. After dabbling in entrepreneurship, interactive media, and journalism, he moved to Silicon Valley to build analytics applications at scale at Ning and LinkedIn. He lives on the ocean in Pacifica, California with his wife Kate and two fuzzy dogs.

Colophon

The animal on the cover of *Agile Data Science* is a silvery marmoset (*Mico argentatus*). These small New World monkeys live in the eastern parts of the Amazon rainforest and Brazil. Despite their name, silvery marmosets can range in color from near-white to dark brown. Brown marmosets have hairless ears and faces and are sometimes referred to as bare-ear marmosets. Reaching an average size of 22 cm, marmosets are about the size of squirrels, which makes their travel through tree canopies and dense vegetation very easy. Silvery marmosets live in extended families of around twelve, where all the members help care for the young. Marmoset fathers carry their infants around during the day and return them to the mother every two to three hours to be fed. Babies wean from their mother's milk at around six months and full maturity is reached at one to two years old. The marmoset's diet consists mainly of sap and tree gum. They use their sharp teeth to gouge holes in trees to reach the sap, and will occasionally eat fruit, leaves, and insects as well. As the deforestation of the rainforest continues, however, marmosets have begun to eat food crops grown by people; as a result, many farmers view them as pests. Large-scale extermination programs are underway in agricultural areas, and it is still unclear what impact this will have on the overall silvery marmoset population. Because of their small size and mild disposition, marmosets are regularly used as subjects of medical research. Studies on the fertilization, placental development, and embryonic stem cells of marmosets may reveal the causes of developmental problems and genetic disorders in humans. Outside of the lab, marmosets are popular at zoos because they are diurnal (active during daytime) and full of energy; their long claws mean they can quickly move around in trees, and both males and females communicate with loud vocalizations.

The cover image is from Lydekker's *Royal Natural History*. The cover fonts are URW Typewriter and Guardian Sans. The text font is Adobe Minion Pro; the heading font is Adobe Myriad Condensed; and the code font is Dalton Maag's Ubuntu Mono.

Get even more for your money.

Join the O'Reilly Community, and register the O'Reilly books you own. It's free, and you'll get:

- $4.99 ebook upgrade offer
- 40% upgrade offer on O'Reilly print books
- Membership discounts on books and events
- Free lifetime updates to ebooks and videos
- Multiple ebook formats, DRM FREE
- Participation in the O'Reilly community
- Newsletters
- Account management
- 100% Satisfaction Guarantee

Signing up is easy:

1. **Go to: oreilly.com/go/register**
2. **Create an O'Reilly login.**
3. **Provide your address.**
4. **Register your books.**

Note: English-language books only

To order books online:
oreilly.com/store

For questions about products or an order:
orders@oreilly.com

To sign up to get topic-specific email announcements and/or news about upcoming books, conferences, special offers, and new technologies:
elists@oreilly.com

For technical questions about book content:
booktech@oreilly.com

To submit new book proposals to our editors:
proposals@oreilly.com

O'Reilly books are available in multiple DRM-free ebook formats. For more information:
oreilly.com/ebooks

Spreading the knowledge of innovators   oreilly.com

Have it your way.

CPSIA information can be obtained at www.ICGtesting.com
Printed in the USA
LVOW01s1825291013

359127LV00016B/64/P